When Your People Are GRIEVING

"For those encountering, experiencing, and expressing a time of loss, *When Your People Are Grieving* is a comprehensive, insightful, essential manual for the minister of grace. Pastors must make time to immerse themselves in the principles and practice of this work."

—Dr. Griffin Jones, Senior Pastor, Temple Baptist Church, Odessa, Texas

"Harold Ivan Smith delivers a vivid reminder to pastors that a funeral is not just another part of the job. His insights provide inspiration, practicality, and creativity to increase our ability to minister effectively to those who are grieving. You will discover usable illustrations and spiritual formation resources that will strengthen those you lead."

—Larry W. Leonard, Senior Pastor, Highland Park Church of the Nazarene, Lakeland, Florida

"Here is the book pastors have been looking for. Practical, insightful handles for providing the ministry of grace to and with the bereaving flow from the pages."

—Jesse C. Middendorf, Senior Pastor, First Church of the Nazarene, Kansas City, Missouri

"*When Your People Are Grieving* is a tremendous tool for any clergyperson who is ministering to those suffering from loss. Harold Ivan Smith is truly gifted at providing deep spiritual insights for those sacred times of death and grief."

—Rev. Mary Grace Williams, Rector, The Episcopal Church of St. John the Evangelist, Flossmoor, Illinois

"Harold Ivan Smith has given the church a handbook on dealing with the 'soul' issues of grief. Within the pages of this book you will discover the importance of empowering a congregation to assist in the ministry of grief care. I plan to give this book to every caregiver in my local church."

—Dr. Stan Toler, Author and Senior Pastor, Trinity Church of the Nazarene, Oklahoma City, Oklahoma

"In the tradition of Wayne Oates and Thomas Oden, Smith calls for busy CEO pastors to return to their role as 'physician of the soul' in time of crisis, trauma, death, and bereavement. He demonstrates how to be there by providing practical research and resources from the field of death and bereavement for preaching, teaching, bedside presence, graveside service, and postfuneral pastoral care."

—Dr. Michael Christenson, Professor, Drew University, Madison, New Jersey

"This book is a treasure of spiritual wisdom, psychological good sense, and practical guidance for ministers who desire to fulfill their calling to minister to people in their bereavement."

—H. Stephen Shoemaker, Senior Minister, Myers Park Baptist Church, Charlotte, North Carolina

"With the brilliance of a skilled artisan and the tender heart of a caring friend, we have the respected gifts of Harold Ivan Smith that educate, equip, comfort, and as needed, chastise religious leaders to claim their rightful place in the care of the bereaved."

—Dr. Richard B. Gilbert, Executive Dirctor, The World Pastoral Care Center, Elgin, Illinois

When Your People Are
GRIEVING

LEADING IN
TIMES OF LOSS

HAROLD IVAN SMITH

Beacon Hill Press of Kansas City
Kansas City, Missouri

Copyright 2001
by Beacon Hill Press of Kansas City

ISBN 083-411-898X

Printed in the
United States of America

Cover Design: Ted Ferguson

Cover Photos: The Stock Market

Library of Congress Cataloging-in-Publication Data

Smith, Harold Ivan, 1947-
    When your people are grieving : leading in times of loss / Harold Ivan Smith.
        p. cm.
    Includes bibliographical references.
    ISBN 0-8341-1898-X (pbk.)
        1. Church work with the bereaved. 2. Grief—Religious aspects—Christianity. 3. Loss (Psychology)—Religious aspects—Christianity. 4. Pastoral theology. I. Title.

BV4330 .S58 2001
259'.6—dc21

                                                                    2001035489

10   9   8   7   6   5   4   3   2   1

To Dennis and Beulah Apple,
who have taught and continue to teach me
a great deal about bereaving
after the death of their son, Denny.

To Chaplains Jerry Kolb and John Swift
of St. Luke's Hospital, Kansas City,
who have provided me a safe setting
in which to work with the bereaving.

To the late Rev. Eudell Milby,
who modeled pastoral leadership
as pastor of Trinity Church of the Nazarene
Louisville, Kentucky

Contents

Call the Preacher
   and tell him, "Come!"
Death is shambling our lives
   and mocking our faith!

Slice the hope thick.
Do not let it elude us—
   for sorrow has come
   and punctured
   our manicured fantasies
   and nursed dreams.

Preacher, come, sit among us.
   Help us find
   enough courage
   to wrap fingers tightly
   around ancient truths—
   once, far more
   readily believed—
   and ancient truths
   that will become,
   in the days ahead,
   a lifesaver
   for the swells of grief.

Preacher, come, sit a spell
   and tell us
   "God does all things well."
Point us to a future dawn.
Preacher, help us grieve.
                    —Harold Ivan Smith

Introduction
When Your People Are Grieving: Lead

I love funerals. I don't love people dying. I love the opportunity a funeral brings to develop a bond with grievers that lasts a lifetime.
—Dale Galloway

A couple spent a weekend with a young grieving widow. Through the course of the weekend they tried to hear her grief, but—well—it was time for her to move on. She should count her blessings: she was not destitute and had two healthy children. She should look on the bright side! "You're young," they pointedly reminded her. "You'll remarry. You may even have more children."

The widow was angered that they would dare suggest such a thing. To a thank-you note acknowledging the presents for the children she added these words: "You must know that I consider my life to be over. And I will spend the rest of my life waiting for it really to be over" (Bradlee, 1995, p. 262).

These were tough words that widow wrote in January 1964. She would have passed a polygraph test—she truly believed her life was over. But it was *not* over for Jackie Kennedy, widow of United States President John F. Kennedy, who was assassinated in November 1963. Nor is it over for the grievers who sit in your office or talk to you in a hallway, in a coffee shop, or on the telephone.

As a caregiver, you offer neither platitudes nor certaintudes. Pastor leaders repeatedly offer the hint of a tomorrow!

Reaved

To be bereaved is to be *reaved*. "Reave" is a wonderful archaic English word that means to break, plunder, rob, tear apart, or deprive one of something. Thus, the griever can say, "I am reaved" and be precise because he or she has been reaved of a loved one and the tomorrows that would have been shared with that loved one. Many people who will look to you for leadership following a loss believe their world has been torn apart. It has been changed forever. And while they do want to believe in the resurrection of believers, many do not have the courage to wrap their fingers tightly around that cherished promise of the Christian faith.

Once upon a time it would have been taken for granted that a pastor's responsibility as shepherd and "curer of souls" would be to be present for the griever. The Gallup Organization reported in 1997 that only one in three believe a member of the clergy could be comforting in a time of loss (Gallup, 1997, p. 7); only one in four say that it is "very important" for a member of the clergy to be on hand when a person is dying (p. 13). Death and dying have become very secularized in this country. Many would more likely turn to a counselor or psychologist than a minister. Yet the hunger is there. Consider the success of *Tuesdays with Morrie,* which has been perched on the best-seller list for more than three years in a nation that the author says has become "a Persian bazaar of self-help" (Albom, 1997, p. 65), or *How We Die,* by Sherwin Nuland, which won a National Book of the Year award.

> **Grief or trauma produce states of mind and emotion that call for spiritual counsel.**
> —Marshall Shelley

It is the spiritual helper who repeatedly points the griever to another perspective who gives hope. It is the godly minister who helps grievers continue to love and live in anticipation of reunion.

This darkness called grief will not be permanent.

Sometimes it takes a pastor-leader to first grasp that reality.

Wonderful Counselor is one of Isaiah's definitions of the One who calls us and accompanies us (9:6). Ironically, many who have been called to represent the Wonderful Counselor often say, "I'm no counselor" in this era of an abundance of skilled professional counselors, especially Christian ones. Some pastors have begun to assume that grief is a psychological issue best dealt with by professionals.

No—grief is a significant *spiritual* issue. The One who calls you would say to you as clearly as he said to Peter that day along the seashore, "Take care of my sheep" (John 21:16). Rarely will the "sheep" be more at risk than in bereavement.

The Old Testament prophet Ezekiel indicted shepherds with the pronouncement, "You do not take care of the flock" (Ezek. 34:3). Specifically he charged,

- You have not strengthened the weak.
- You have not healed the sick.
- You have not bound up the injured.
- You have not brought back the lost.
- You have ruled them harshly and brutally.

The result of inattention by the shepherd in Ezekiel's day as well as today? "They were scattered because there was no shepherd, and when they were scattered they became food for all the wild animals" (Ezek. 34:5). Using Paul's words from Eph. 4:14, they were "blown here and there by every wind of teaching."

What is a pastor to do?

The *Manual of the Church of the Nazarene* defines as one of the duties of a pastor "to comfort those who mourn" (413.6, 1997—2001, p. 173), appropriate for pastor of any Christian denomination. That's it—five words. In essence, the ball is in your court to figure out what that means. I am reminded of Ed Koch, former mayor of New York City, who continually asked while in office, "How am I doing?" What does it mean to "comfort those who mourn"? Many pastors would answer, "It depends upon the situation."

Pray this prayer with me:

Wonderful Counselor, Comforter, Friend of grievers,
How am I doing as a shepherd?
How am I caring for Your sheep who are reaved?
Spend some moments with this prayer before reading further.

This book is about answering a question: "How am I doing as a pastor?" The grief of your parishioners is as clear a call to servanthood as a fire bell summoning volunteer firemen. A sensitivity to "nowness" is imperative. As a pastor, how do you lead in the immediacy of a loss, particularly a "this makes no sense" loss? Maybe even more important, how do you lead *long-term* when grief settles in?

This book offers pastors several useful tools:

- Quotations are provided for use in preaching, teaching, and counseling.
- Each chapter ends with a "story that will preach" designed to help you feed your sheep. Through preaching and teaching, the pastor-leader prepares his or her people for the inevitable pilgrimage through the valley of the shadow of death. Some of the stories can be used as starters for funeral sermons.
- Resources from the latest research in the field of death and bereavement are listed. I will introduce you to the work of leading thanatologists (specialists in grief) and clinicians: Alan Wolfelt, Bill Worden, Terese Rando, Tony Walter, and Robert Neimeyer. Few of them have written specifically to pastors, so I have lifted salient points from their research and repackaged them for busy pastors. Wayne Oates advises pastors, "Having inherited such a ministry, you can conserve your spiritual birthright and add to it your own personal spiritual fortune by assimilating all that modern research has to offer in discipline and technique and by understanding Biblical truth in terms of human needs" (1982, p. 63).

- Each chapter ends with a spiritual formation exercise. Some pastors read with one goal: "On to the next chapter." I hope you will *make time* to experience each exercise. Pastor-leaders must lead from well-stocked resources. These experiences will help you process the material in the chapter. It is a way to ask, *God, what do You want to say to me through what I have read?*

In this book I will deliberately use the word bereav*ing* rather than the more traditional word bereav*ed*. The word bereav*ed* communicates what has occurred in the past, that this loss is simply something to get over. Our time-focused hurry-up culture wants brief grief or "grief lite." It rigorously communicates, "Stay busy! Get over it! Get on with life!" We shame the loved one daring to experience thorough grief: "He wouldn't want you carrying on like this, would he?" In a culture that asks, if at all, "How are you holding up?" many only want to hear, "Fine, fine. Thank you for asking." Little surprise that the bereaving eventually follow the script, "I'm fine."

A griever will not get over a loss. The reaving is permanent. Bereaving is in the present—ongoing. The question is, "What will the grieving individual do with his or her loss?" Because so many will camouflage their grief, it may turn destructive. Some will "deconstruct" their belief in God—after all, a "good" God would not have allowed this loss.

A tale of two widows

Perhaps you have visited the Winchester Mansion in San Jose, California, built by Sarah Winchester, heir to the Winchester rifle fortune. Sarah's one-month-old daughter died in 1866, and her husband, William, died in 1881. In her distress following her husband's death, she sought out a medium, who informed her that because her vast wealth came from the Winchester rifle invented by her father-in-law, that device had been instrumental in the killing of native Americans and animals such as the buffalo; her fortune was therefore "blood-soaked." Sarah decided she must protect herself and atone for these many deaths by building a castle. As long as it was under construction, she convinced herself, she would live. The moment construction stopped, night or day, she would die.

For 40 years, seven days a week, on holidays and around the clock, craftsmen worked, some days building, other days tearing down until at one point the house had 750 rooms. In today's money Sarah Winchester spent perhaps $20,000,000 (Burgess, 1989, pp. 40-44).

I've often wondered, "What if she had talked to a kind pastor-leader instead of the medium?" Is it possible that a pastor failed her and that the hurt influenced her to seek out the medium? How might Sarah's life have been different with the influence of a griever-sensitive pastor? Admittedly a favorite California tourist attraction would not exist. Perhaps an institution or institutions of the kingdom of God would have been blessed by her generosity. (Some of the Winchester money through another heir, Olive Winchester, went to Pasadena College, forerunner of Point Loma Nazarene University in San Diego.)

Whenever I think of Sarah, I also think of her contemporary, Louise Newcomb in New Orleans, who also lost a husband and a child. However, Mrs. Newcomb in her bereaving poured her resources into educating other people's daughters. The result: Sophie Newcomb College, which became part of Tulane University.

Both widows were devastated by their losses of husbands and daughters, but their choices led to different responses.

You—as a pastor-leader in a therapeutic age— can make a difference, a marvelous difference with unforseen consequences.

One of the great tributes to a pastor is when a griever says, "I don't know how we would be making it through this without our pastor."

My hope is that resources in this book will make this a common expression in your ministry as a pastor, a shepherd, that on your busiest day when what Robert Neimeyer calls "the unwelcome intruder" (1998, p. 41) comes, you'll remember you are called to be a servant.

> **If you stop being a servant, you stop being a minister. You don't have a ministry left. You have lost your authenticity.**
> **—Dale Galloway**

Some pastor-leaders are good at conducting funerals. Still, conducting these services is an acquired art rather than a skill. After a particular funeral you may reflect and wince at your own insensitivity. Certainly there will be funerals that pastors have not had time to prepare for, so they promise, *God, please help me, and I'll never be so insensitive again.* In fact, some unforgettable act of insensitivity may have led you to purchase this book. But despite a negative assessment of performance, sometimes at the cemetery or afterward over potato salad and chicken that the ladies of the church have prepared, or weeks later at the grocery, someone will likely say, "Pastor, you really helped me that day." And for the life of you, you'll not be able to recall anything you said that could have been helpful.

The Holy Spirit can take the words of the insensitive and the inexperienced for His glory. But something rather extraordinary can happen when He works through a prepared vessel.

The promise of the hymn "In the Garden" is as true for those who lead funerals as for those on the front row: "And He walks with me, and He talks with me." Jesus promised, "Anyone who has faith in me will do what I have been doing. He will do even greater things than these" (John 14:12).

Wise pastor-leaders have learned that grievers can teach us. We can learn from their experience if we have a servant's learning heart. Pastor-leaders have a responsibility to "understand the effects of this loss even if we are not able truly to understand the experience itself" (Long, 1992, p. 51). The wise pastor never forgets this assessment by James Miller:

"Even if you have been through *other* losses in your life, you have never made your way through *this* loss" (Miller, 2000, p. 10).

In preparing this introduction, I dusted off a copy of Joseph Bayly's *The View from the Hearse* (1969), written after he buried his third son. In it he cautions Christians, "We are most likely to be helpful with an economy of words" (p. 40). A psychiatrist friend shared this insight with Bayly: "When Job's friends came to see him after his children died and he had suffered in so many other ways, they missed the opportunity to go down in history as uniquely sensitive and understanding. There they sat on the ground with him for seven days and nights, and they didn't say a word, because they saw how utterly grief-stricken he was. But then they begin to talk and spoiled it all" (p. 40).

Bayly concludes, "Sensitivity in the presence of grief should usually make us more silent, more listening" (p. 40).

You may have an opportunity to go down in a family's history, in stories passed from generation to generation, as "uniquely sensitive and understanding." But some opportunities come disguised as messes!

Evaluation in ministry must be beyond the fallible judgment of statistic keepers. The sad truth, according to Kent and Barbara Hughes, is this:

It is possible to pastor a huge church and not love people!

It is possible to design and preside over perfectly conceived and executed worship services and not love people!

It is possible to preach insightful, biblical, sermons and not love people! (Hughes, 1987, p. 59).

I would ask:

Is it possible to conduct smooth funerals *and not love people?*

Is it possible to take stories about the deceased and weave them masterfully into a funeral sermon or eulogy *and not love people?*

Is it possible to say the right words at a committal *and not love people?*

Is it possible to really comfort the bereaving *and not love people?*

Remember the conclusion of the onlookers observing Jesus near Lazarus' grave: "See how he *loved* him!" (John 11:36, emphasis added).

We have heard much in recent years about the need to be "seeker-sensitive." There is an equal need to be "griever-sensitive."

I first began to construct the image of griever-sensitive pastor-leader while listening to Tony Campolo tell a story about his pastor friend who has the reputation of conducting funerals that other pastors will not conduct. One day Tony asked him, "Anything interesting happen today?" The funeral was routine and by the book, except for the fact that the mourners "stared straight ahead with glassy, unfocused eyes" (Campolo, 1988, p. 19). The pastor reported, "I did what I was supposed to do. I read some scripture and said some prayers. I made the kind of remarks that ministers are supposed to make when they really don't know the dead person."

At the cemetery, the pastor concluded with prayer and walked away but realized that none of the 25 or so mourners had moved from the grave. "I turned and walked back to them and asked if there was anything more I could do for them." One man said, "When I got up this morning to come to this funeral, I was looking forward to somebody reading the Twenty-third Psalm to me. I really like that Psalm, and I figured that they always read the Twenty-third Psalm at funerals. You didn't read the Twenty-third Psalm" (p. 20).

So Campolo's friend read Psalm 23 aloud. When another man requested a particular Bible passage about nothing being able to separate us from the love of God, the pastor read the 8th chapter of Romans. Signs of emotion slowly began to show on these grievers' faces. Request after request was verbalized until an hour had passed. I'm reasonably sure that the funeral home had paid for the basic "get 'em in the ground" stranger's funeral. But this griever-sensitive pastor saw and seized an opportunity.

What would you have done? Opportunities for leadership come to pastors in unlikely places, including cemeteries. Again I ask, What would you have done in a moment that cried out for sensitive pastoral leadership?

A pastor-leader must offer help, not because you understand this particular loss, but because in this particular grief you are Christ's ambassador.

In Alistair Cooke's biography of Edward VIII, the British monarch who abdicated to marry an American woman in 1937, these words summarized his brief kingship: "He was at his very best only when the going was good" (1977, p. 82). May it be said of you as a pastor, "He [She] was at his [her] very best when times were dark."

1
Why Pastoral Care?

*Probably there is no greater need for a pastor's ministry in a
person's life than when that person experiences the death
of a loved one. No other opportunity in life gives the
pastor a better chance to minister to people.*
—Robert Anderson

Key Point Summary
No other opportunity in life gives the pastor a better opportunity to lead people not only in the rituating but also in the long days of bereaving. In both, outsiders witness the leadership skills or lack of skills of a pastor.

Death happens

Approximately 2.3 million persons die in the United States in a given year (Wright, 1998, p. 393). Each of those deaths theoretically creates an opportunity for pastoral leadership and care and for a congregational care response

- at the time of dying
- in the transition between death and the rituals
- during the rituating

Jane Jones, age 45, has died. By relationship (husband, friend, and so on) identify the potential grievers whom you, as a pastor, may meet at a visitation or funeral/memorial service:

1. _____	7. _____
2. _____	8. _____
3. _____	9. _____
4. _____	10. _____
5. _____	11. _____
6. _____	12. _____

- through pastoral bereavement care to the survivors, sometimes long after the death—in the words of title, *After the Flowers Have Gone* (Decker, 1973).

The potential recipients of pastoral care are as follows:

- the immediate family: spouse, sons, daughters, grandchildren, siblings, parents, grandparents, aunts, uncles, cousins, nieces, nephews

and

- friends, colleagues, neighbors, work associates, fellow church members

Lageman (1986, pp. 16-22) identifies the groups who attend visitations and funerals.

Five Groups Under the Umbrella Term "Griever"

Level 1: The grieving inner core	**family + intimate friends**
Level 2: The functional others	**close friends**
Level 3: The occasional others	**present to fulfill an obligation i.e., casual friends/business associates**
Level 4: The general others	
Level 5: The marginal others	**acquaintances**

In the case of tragedies, I would add a Level 6: The *curious* others. Suppose we arbitrarily say that a dozen persons are directly influenced by each death. That translates into 21.6 million individuals directly impacted by death in a year's time. The Columbine High School shooting (in Littleton, Colorado) or the bombing of the Murrah Federal Building in Oklahoma City leaves whole communities, and a nation, grieving. Moreover, people are impacted by the anniversaries of deaths.

Particular grievers will be ambushed by media stories of similar deaths.

In too many cases, grievers wonder, "How can my pastor not know what to say or how to support me? Of all the people in my life, the pastor is supposed to know what to say and do at a time like this." That's the purpose of this resource: to offer resources to today's busy clergy who know that death has a way of making shambles of one's schedule and priorities for the day.

I have not forgotten a friend, Paul, at his first church, who conducted three funerals in the first 10 days after graduating from seminary! How to do funerals well and how to provide leadership to a grieving family, friends, congregation, and community was not adequately covered in seminary classwork. Paul called a senior pastor of a large church and pleaded, "Tell me what to do." Maybe he should have asked, "Tell me how to lead this congregation in grief."

Pastoral care as leadership

As a leader in a faith community, a pastor is expected to speak authentically to and be available "to receive" (Rohr, 2000, p. 111) the laments, questions, observations, heartaches, and narratives of grievers, even those that cannot be verbalized. Pastors are expected to lead, in the phrase of the hymn, "whate'er betide" (Martin, 1904/1993, p. 107).

Think of some of the disasters that have commanded the attention of the nation in recent years. Think of pastors who suddenly found themselves dealing with not only distraught family and friends but also, perhaps through sound bytes or live coverage of a ritual, speaking to thou-

> **Always be prepared to give an answer to everyone who asks you to give the reason for the hope that you have.**
> **—1 Pet. 3:15**

sands, to millions, in many cases with little preparation time. Many Americans believe an act of outrageous violence or terrorism could occur in their community. Could your community be touched next? Could the next tragedy statistics be members of your congregation?

Take a moment and look out your study window to the church parking lot. Can you imagine CNN satellite trucks or news cam crews parked there? Few pastors can. Jim Henry, pastor of First Baptist Church in Orlando, Florida, certainly didn't that October 1999 morning. He had just spent time with an associate reviewing the progress of a building project. Minutes later, Henry's secretary stuck her head into his office and said, "It's Randall James, and it's an emergency."

"'Emergency.' How can it be an emergency? I just talked with him two minutes ago." (In the age of the cell phone, emergencies seem to happen much more quickly.)

Randall James entered the office to break the news that professional golfer Payne Stewart was on board a private jet flying over the Midwest on automatic pilot. Apparently no one on board was alive. Suddenly a huge leadership crisis dropped into this busy pastor's lap.

James recalls Pastor Henry's initial response: "He appeared broken at just the prospect all of this could be true. I had kind of a feeling of shock. I was scared and felt a big knot in my stomach. And I could tell Jim felt the same way" (Guest, 2000, p. 28).

Agendas, priorities, schedules for that pastor and the staff were turned upside down. Although Stewart was not a member of First Baptist, his children attended their school, and Stewart was a lead donor on the church's project to develop a first-class athletic program. Still, like

> I would say in all my years of pastoring, Payne's death, combined with the memorial service that followed, has been the most dramatic impact of affecting other people across the board, of any single event I can remember. . . . The drama—the trauma, the thing of so many people remembering where they were and what they were doing when it happened—was unique.
>
> —Jim Henry (Guest, 2000, p. 29)

many people these days who are reluctant to join a church, Stewart considered First Baptist "his" church. Many, including the biggest names in professional golf—would be looking to the pastoral leadership of this church in the days ahead.

But this was early in the pastoral drama. By the time of the memorial service, 18 television satellite trucks were in the parking lot, and reporters and camera crews were everywhere on the church campus. CNN decided to broadcast the service live.

No problem, Pastor—you've done funerals for 40 years!

Then there's another perspective. Consider a young woman watching the CNN coverage of the plane carrying her husband and friends. Soon girlfriends began arriving at Tracey Stewart's home as well as a representative from the Professional Golf Association, then some from the church, pastors Jim Henry and J. B. Collingsworth. Pastor Henry was with Tracey when the news report came in that the plane had run out of fuel and crashed into a field in South Dakota. The wife, the pastor, and the world learned simultaneously.

Soon the children arrived home, and Tracey broke the news to them. Then she asked Pastor Henry to pray with them. As a pastor, you, too, have had such moments, although perhaps not of this media magnitude, haven't you?

Being there for the dying and the grieving

Whatever their title and credentials, religious leaders have historically been expected to "be there" for the dying and the grieving. Clergymembers are expected to provide spiritual leadership in the unbelievable moments, traumas, and tragedies of life. And make no mistake—even Grandma's quiet death in a nursing home has elements of trauma for someone.

In the great moments of life—births, marriages, deaths—people want a touch of the special, of the mystical, of the communal. They want leadership, not "Well, let's just try to get through this the best way we can." While a funeral director will take care of many of the details, the pastor will set the tone.

One Southern hymn captures the reality well: "I won't have to cross Jordan alone." No one should have to grieve a loved one's crossing alone either. Certainly opportunities to accompany the dying and the grieving come in inopportune moments. Whether roused from a deep sleep, sermon preparation, moments with a spouse, or relaxing with children on a ball field, ministers find themselves immediately immersed, in one pastor's summation, "knee deep in grief." There is little time to check schedule books. Death takes priority—everything else becomes secondary. In fact, many find death the definitive moment in pastoral care.

Someone once reprimanded famed Episcopal pastor Phillips Brooks because he had spent time with a dying person who was not a member of his congregation, thereby delaying the start of a social function, "Why didn't you send someone else?" "He called for me," Brooks noted, ending the conversation.

In the crises of life, many want a representative of God present. In some instances they want not just a generic representative but a particular one: *you,* not as a spectator, but as an active participant—one among us. In fact, often denominational affiliations, credentials, and titles mean little to the grieving. The minister is recognized as a representative of God in the "I can't believe this is happening to us" moment, in the "Let this cup pass" experience. The news reports that United States President John Kennedy had been shot in Dallas in November 1963 became even more sobering when network anchors reported that he had received the Roman Catholic last rites from a priest. Very rarely does anyone say at the time of death, "Quick—call a psychotherapist!" or "Call a social worker!" Most frequently, the request goes out for a minister.

A wise veteran pastor describes one interruptible moment:

> I had the strongest nudge: Go to the Andersons' house. I looked at my sermon notes and thought, "I'll go as soon as I finish this." But the nudge became stronger: *Go to the Andersons'—now.* I went, and all the way over there I reminded the Lord that I was overwhelmed with all that was on me. When I arrived, nothing seemed to be out of the ordinary. I was sitting there drinking coffee and chatting with them when the police officer knocked on the door. I was there when their "Oh, God—no!" moment began. For a long time I was troubled by the fact that I almost missed that opportunity—not by wasting time, but by doing something important.

Paul's instruction is still timely, across all denominational and faith backgrounds, beyond job descriptions and expectations: "As we have opportunity, let us do good to all people, especially to those who belong to

> **When the funeral service is over, your pastoral work . . . is just beginning.**
> —Richard D. Dobbins

the family of believers" (Gal. 6:10). The reality may be that the opportunity is with individuals who have been wounded by other pastors.

Pastors also will have opportunity to "do good" to the growing numbers of persons who define themselves as spiritual but not religious who become part of our care for the moment of a funeral. Some you may never see again—but in the immediacy of this service or the next few days, you are or could be the pastor—*their* pastor. I think Paul's words can be phrased like this: "As you *make* opportunity" or "as you *take advantage of* the opportunity," however slight, do good.

Grievers Who Fall Through the Cracks

- those who do not have a church "home"
- those who have stopped attending a church because of a congregational situation or tension
- those who do not speak English or Spanish
- those whose loved one died away from their home community while traveling on business or vacation
- those whose loved one was undergoing treatment in a specialty medical center in another city
- those who have recently relocated or are in transition
- those who have been abused by organized religion
- those members of highly dysfunctional families
- those who have been marginalized by society
- those who cannot be involved in a church due to health reasons or disabilities
- those with mental disorders and disabilities
- young children
- ex's: spouses, in-laws

Paul's instructions also remind that although an individual pastor responds to "as *you* have opportunity" pastors represent not spiritual Lone Rangers, but a chosen, called profession: "let *us* do good to all people" (emphasis added). These days, that could mean "let us do good" to some folks who are candidates for the Jerry Springer Show.

Those who do not receive pastoral care

When there is inadequate pastoral care during the immediacy of the death, some build barriers to future pastoral care even if it should be offered. Inadequate care in one death will influence expectations in subsequent deaths. In these hectic never-enough-hours-in-a-day-to-get-it-all-done days, some pastors, especially in metropolitan areas, ask, "Is this dying person or bereaved person a member of *my* congregation?" Some busy pastors reason, "The hospital chaplain can handle this one." Other pastors, however, mercifully welcome the stranger, or, as one pastor termed it, the "not-yet friend." They realize this is *someone's* loved one. Indeed, some pastoral opportunities come at the invitation of a funeral director who, having observed the pastor work with other families, trusts him to "do a good job" with this family.

Historically, faith communities have taken responsibility for giving even strangers "a decent burial," even indigent strangers (Pohl, 1999, p. 167). The author of Hebrews counsels, "Do not neglect to show hospitality to strangers" (Heb. 13:2, NASB). But many have higher expectations for pastoral and congregational care from the church in which one has membership, regularly attends, or financially supports. This is becoming more of an issue in this era when people have multiple congregational affiliations.

Managed pastoral care

"Managed health care" is a reality in today's world. One nurse defines managed care this way: "When you're done with our care—we're done with you!" As I've listened to individuals evaluate pastoral care during bereavement, I'm coming to believe that rationed, minimal pastoral care is no longer rare, but common. Certainly I experienced that when my mother was dying and after she died. One woman summed up the absence of care: "Let's just put it this way: the pastor did not go out of his way to help us."

Many overlook the lack of pastoral care with these words: "The pastor is so busy." And some pastors are busy wrestling with the tyranny of the important. My father's pastor explained why he had not visited the funeral home during the two days of visitation: "Your father is being buried above ground. Well, the *Manual* doesn't have any provisions for above-ground burials, so I've been researching what to do."

Candidates being ordained in the United Methodist tradition hear these words:

"Remember that you are called to serve rather than to be served . . . to look after the concerns of Christ above all" (*The United Methodist Book of Worship*, 1992, pp. 688-89). Paraphrasing Paul's words, "Your schedule is not your own; you were called at a price" (1 Cor. 6:19, author's paraphrase). What many would label an interruption is an opportunity.

I do not intend this to be an indictment of all pastors and pastoral care givers. I have heard numerous stories of clergy who regularly go the second mile (and third and fourth miles), are accessible to the family at all hours of the day and night, even commuting to be with family when a

> ### Pastors Who Are
> ### Effective with Grievers
> - are never in a hurry, never watch the clock
> - have an ability to "be with" the griever
> - are willing to hear out the griever's struggling lament
> - are comfortable with the silences and pauses
> - are comfortable with voiced anger: expressed at God, at the doctors, at the deceased, at the church, at a drunken driver, and so on
> - make grievers feel more comfortable
> - take offering pastoral care seriously
> - give parishioners permission to grieve thoroughly
> - listen all the way to the end of grievers' sentences—even the ones that don't have periods

loved one was receiving care in a distant medical specialty center. I think it would not abuse Jesus' intent to paraphrase His words, "I was hungry and you gave me something to eat" (Matt. 25:35), to read, "I was grieving and you visited me."

Wise pastors do not respond to the needs of the bereaving with prepackaged "for presentation in this situation" responses. Even veteran clergy will have moments in which they do not know what to do or say or how to respond. While I was on the staff of Point Loma Nazarene University, a string of deaths (including the president's) devastated the campus community. I've never forgotten going to chapel after yet another untimely death, expecting that if anyone would know something appropriate to say, university chaplain Reuben Welch would.

Naturally, we sang and someone prayed. Then it was time for Reuben. In a brutally honest yet caring way, he said, "If I knew what to say, I would say it. If I knew what to sing, I would sing it. But, folks, I do not know what to say or sing!" Then after a pause, he began reading John's words, "Let not your heart be troubled" (John 14:1, KJV).

That was a moment of great pastoral leadership and vulnerability to a distressed academic community. Reuben didn't fake it. He wasn't overly creative or innovative. He was caring. I vividly remember that chapel experience two decades later.

Leaders take every opportunity seriously

Generally, few pastors get a second chance with the same family to redeem poor pastoral care leadership following a death. In the days before a pending death, family members may say, "I'll tell you who is *not* doing the funeral." Thomas Oden stresses the historic role of pastor in offering spiritual hospitality to the dying and to the bereaving:

For persons experienced in ministry, however, the tender, quiet, heavily weighted moments of ministering to people amid death may prove to be among the most meaningful events of a year's work, those most often dreamed about, those remembered years later, those that best offer opportunities to mediate God's love to human brokenness, those that infuse the rest of ministry with profound inconspicuous significance" *(1983, p. 296).*

The pastor and opportunity windows

Pastors assess opportunities through the lens of their strengths. Some pastors are pulpiteers; others are administrators. Some have great leadership skills; others are teachers.

Some can shape a vision; others maintain a predecessor's vision. Some are great at ritualizing; others are in their prime as fund-raisers and vision-renewers. Rarely do church board members while interviewing perspective pastors ask, "How are you at conducting funerals?" Pastors in interviews are rarely asked, "Tell us about your grief care skills."

Some pastors have great difficulty conducting funerals, sometimes because of unprocessed bereavement of their own. Today pastors of large churches routinely delegate funeral and grief-related pastoral care to associates. The issue of who gets a funeral conducted by a senior pastor can have ethical implications. In one megachurch I asked, "How much money would an individual have to give in order for the senior pastor to do the funeral?" Staff members laughed, then were silent. Finally one answered, "A lot."

> The experienced minister knows that the times of approaching death and bereavement are exceptional opportunities for spiritual growth. Sensitive care is required to nurture them toward their fullest potentiality and not let them become an occasion for stumbling. They have great potentiality for demonic as well as creative growth.
> —Thomas C. Oden, 1983, p. 297

Sometimes a pastor's strengths are not clearly evident to me. When I have questioned parishioners about a pastor's effectiveness of gifts, I've often heard, "Oh, when my wife died [my husband died, my son was killed, my mother died], the pastor was right there for [with] us." Not a few parishioners have added, "I don't know how we would have made it through all that without our pastor."

Pastor-leaders have developed a keen partnership with the Holy Spirit to recognize "opportunity" moments.

When the pastor is an active, rather than occasional, companion who walks alongside grieving parishioners, many will overlook all manner of homiletical or personal inadequacies in a pastor who is in deed, in crisis, a pastor.

Oden argues the pastor's task is to be a good steward of such sacred moments.

This is particularly true when family members and friends, and perhaps the pastor, are already emotionally and physically exhausted after tense hours or weary days in hospital waiting rooms and corridors, a nursing home, or a private home during roller-coaster hours of an impending death.

In other cases, when the patient is at death's door and the pastor is summoned, or when the family is in shock, a pastor's care in such moments becomes an important element in the family narrative: "He [She] was here for us when we needed a pastor." More so for the pastor who may be juggling multiple congregational griefs and other demands for intense pastoral care. Many pastors have experienced the death of a key member during a building program, financial drought, or church tension.

Botched opportunities for ministry happen

Ministry opportunities are occasionally missed or completely botched up. But once is too much if it involves *your* mother, *your* child, or *your* spouse. Somehow the promise to "do better next time" falls flat.

The Goal of Pastoral Ministry

To provide good stewardship of the opportunities as a pastor to lead people not only in the ritualing but also in the long days of bereaving.

A Spiritual Formation Exercise

1. Spend some moments with Gal. 6:10—"As we have opportunity, let us do good to all people, especially to those who belong to the family of believers." Read the passage a second time. Slowly. Let your finger follow the text. This time instead of reading "As we have opportunity," read "As we *make* opportunity . . ."
2. Now read this passage in *The Living Bible*—"Whenever we can we should always be kind to everyone, and especially to our Christian brothers."
3. Pause. Ask God to speak to you through these words of Scripture.
4. Think about an experience in dealing with a "stranger" in grief. In what ways did you show kindness? Audit your pastoral leadership.

5. Imagine that you are the griever. What acts of pastoral kindness would you appreciate?
6. Carlyle Marney once noted, "God will use any handle to get hold of somebody" (cited in Willimon, 2000, p. 56). What does this observation by a veteran pastor say to you?
7. Sing this verse of the hymn "I Would Be True":

> *I would be prayerful thro' each busy moment.*
> *I would be constantly in touch with God.*
> *I would be tuned to hear His slightest whisper.*
> *I would have faith to keep the path Christ trod.*
> *I would have faith to keep the path Christ trod.*
>   —Howard A. Walter

That path is filled with the constant interruption of demands and requests from those you need to help in Jesus' name.

A Story That Will Preach

Rev. Thomas Nelson faced a decision one cold winter day. He was conducting a graveside service for a stranger. No one had come to the funeral home to pay respects; now no one had come to the cemetery. Nelson conferred with the funeral director. Why not bury the aged veteran and get out of the cold? Still they hesitated. Just before the announced service time for the committal, a car pulled to the curb of the section, and an elderly gentleman got out and walked into the tent and sat down. After concluding a brief ritual of committal, Rev. Nelson walked over to the sole mourner. "Mr. President, why are you here? It's cold and bitter. Did you know this gentleman?"

Harry S. Truman looked at the casket of a World War I comrade and replied, "Pastor, I never forget a friend!" (McCullough, 1992, p. 985).

One can only imagine the ramifications had Nelson proceeded and had former President Truman arrived to find his friend already buried. The story illustrates the point that whether a funeral is large or small, even with only one mourner, it is an opportunity to be a pastor and a leader.

A Leadership Decision

As a result of reflecting on my reading of the chapter, I want to

1. _____

2. _____

2
The Leadership Model of Ebed-Melech

Two life moments are unparalled in awakening a sense of awe: be-holding a birth, and standing in the presence of death.
—Thomas C. Oden, 1983, p. 293

Key Point Summary
Ministry with the dying and the grieving must never be routine or be taken for granted. Ministry with the bereaving is an opportunity to lead.

As a pastor, you may have buried many elderly mothers—but for someone, this is *his or her* elderly mother, and it just might be the first time he or she has ever lost a loved one. Some may have experienced other deaths, but this particular death is different. Your presence in previous grief doesn't count. What counts is how you offer care in this current grief experience.

Grievers want three things from a pastor:
- competence
- presence
- sensitivity

This can best be demonstrated by an example of lived-out risky servanthood found in the Old Testament when a prophet, Jeremiah, desperately needed hospitality.

> You only get one chance to make a good first impression when called upon to help families manage significant loss. Your first few moments with them can lay a foundation for hope or alienate them from the One who is our hope. . . . There is no such thing as a routine crisis intervention.
> —Dan S. Lloyd, 1997, p. 12

The background for the opportunity to lead

Jeremiah found himself in a cistern as a penalty for predicting the fall of Jerusalem to the Babylonians in 587 B.C. Who knows what would have happened had a Cushite eunuch named Ebed-Melech not intervened with sensitivity, competence, and presence? Learning of the ill treatment of Jeremiah and cognizant that Jeremiah could die in that cistern, Ebed-Melech stepped into a leadership role and challenged King Zedekiah, "These men have acted wickedly in all they have done to Jeremiah" (Jer. 38:9), which was only a thin step from indicting the king for approving the scheme in the first place.

Jeremiah, Ebed-Melech insisted, "will starve to death when there is no longer any bread in the city" (v. 9), which suggested that Jeremiah had been correct all along: Jerusalem would fall. Ebed-Melech must have been persuasive, because Zedekiah overrode his leadership council and ordered the eunuch, "Take thirty men from here with you and lift Jeremiah the prophet out of the cistern" (v. 10).

Interestingly, Ebed-Melech did not sprint for the cistern. Rather, he headed to the royal storage room to requisition old rags and worn-out clothes. Then, with resources, he went to Jeremiah prepared. When he dropped the rope, he instructed Jeremiah, "Put these old rags and worn-out clothes under your arms to pad the ropes" (v. 12).

Jeremiah had been lowered into the cistern by ropes. Those ropes had possibly bruised or broken his skin, particularly under his arms. Who knows where the rope had come from and to what bacteria it had been exposed—bacteria now infecting Jeremiah's wounds. Trying to yank Jeremiah quickly out of this cistern before the king might again change his mind could lead to rope burns and possibly, serious infection—even dislocation. So Ebed-Melech wisely and sensitively padded the ropes.

I find in Ebed-Melech a model for pastoral leadership with people in grief. Our goal is not simply to extract people from cisterns called grief as expediently and as efficiently as possible, minimizing our inconvenience—because, to be honest, grief ministry is time-consuming and is emotionally and spiritual draining.

Pastors, like Ebed-Melech, are God's representatives in a particular venue of distress.

The task is to "pad the ropes" of compassion of the congregations we lead) so that the grieving are not further injured by ministry efforts.

The pastor-leader's task is to lead so that the grieving are not further injured by ministry omissions either.

In words that are as relevant as when he penned them, Howard Clinebell Jr. reminds us, "There is no doubt that ministers occupy a central and strategic role as counselors in our society. It is obvious that clergy men [and women] are on the front lines in the struggle to lift the loads of troubled persons" (1966, p. 49).

How? By companioning them through their experience of grief and by witnessing their grief and by receiving their laments and stories. Walter Brueggemann (1978) contends that "prophetic ministry consists in offering an alternative perception of reality and in letting people see their own history in the light of God's freedom" (p. 110) and grace. This is where pastors "try to be of assistance to people struggling with sometimes overwhelming experiences of loss and trauma" (p. 569).

Pastor-leaders realize that this death may reopen previously "closed" griefs.

Most "requests for pastoral care will be made not in a direct manner, but in some disguised form" (p. 120). When one father angrily approached the pastor because the Christmas bulletin noted only who gave the poinsettia plants (rather than the names of the deceased in whose memory they were purchased), the pastor lovingly listened then asked, "This really isn't about poinsettias, is it? It's about how much you miss your son." For others, the "Could you help me?" may be more of a whisper than a shout. This death—and a pastor's response to it—may be the occasion that encourages the person to talk and, in doing so, to voice his or her doubts and confusion and fear.

Indeed, there is initial grief care, which occurs within minutes, hours, or days of the loss. There is also secondary care, which occurs months or even years after the loss. Actually the loss may have occurred during a predecessor's ministry, but something you said in your sermon last Sunday sounded like an invitation this griever needs for revisting the loss. This demonstrates an objection to the stereotypical application of the stages of grief. It is assumed that "doing the stages" leads to recovery, which is more crudely (and it does sound crude to a fresh griever) getting over it and moving on. Rather, grief is cyclical. Under the leadership of the Holy Spirit, grievers return to a grief for another look and for another episode of healing.

Denial ➤ Anger ➤ Bargaining ➤ Acceptance ➤ Growth

Some grievers come with their questions at night, like Nicodemus, when others are not around—with questions well rehearsed. For example, former United States President Dwight D. Eisenhower played golf on several occasions with evangelist Billy Graham. At one point, his need for pastoral care and his belief that Graham could be trusted led him to quiz the evangelist about his concepts of eternal life. Did Graham, Eisenhower asked, really believe in the existence of heaven? Did he believe that people meet up with those they have loved? Graham assured the president that these were not just tradition or myths, but Christ's promises that he believed implicitly. Eisenhower's biographer Geoffrey Perrett (1999) comments, "The terrors of death were undoubtedly assuaged for Eisenhower by the prospect of being reunited with Icky [the president's deceased son] and Ida [the president's mother]" (p. 603). I would point out that the conversation did not come in one of Eisenhower's early talks with Graham, but only after the two had developed a relationship, and that the conversations took place on a golf course rather than in a pastor's study.

Pastor-leaders know that "reachable" moments, particularly with males, come in all sorts of settings.

Billy Graham padded the rope for Dwight David Eisenhower, who never got over the death in 1921 of his three-year-old son.

In a stirring scene in the film *Shadowlands,* about the grief of C. S. Lewis, Lewis sits down with his grieving stepson, Douglas. Mind you, this is one of the foremost theologians of the century, but to Douglas, it is his stepfather. "Jack," he asks, "do you believe in heaven?"

Lewis pauses to reflect and answers, "Yes, I do."

Douglas receives the answer and then says resolutely, "I don't believe in heaven."

Lewis does not whack the boy upside the head. He simply says through his own grief, "That's OK."

Over the years I have been amazed at the response to that film clip by participants in the grief groups I lead at St. Luke's Hospital. They take comfort that Lewis gave the boy permission to have doubts. That dialogue, I suggest, was one of the ways Lewis offered a padded rope to a grieving boy.

Grievers cannot extricate themselves from their cistern called grief. They need a rope. Grievers need someone on the other end to pull. But they really need individuals to pad the ropes—not with pat answers or spiritual clichés or even Scripture promises but with hope.

When noted evangelical author Joseph Bayly lost three sons, he received lots of consolation. One "comforter" strung together Bible verse after verse after verse. Bayly was glad when he left (Bayly, 1979, p. 40). The visitor he most appreciated simply sat with him.

Ezekiel describes a similar experience: "I came to the exiles who lived at Tel Abib near the Kebar River. And there, where they were living, I sat among them for several days— overwhelmed" (Ezek. 3:15).

Many readers of this book, I hope, are young ministers—still intimidated by death and funerals and committals on cold wet days, fearful of saying or doing the wrong thing. Many are like Lorenzo Albacete. Soon after he was ordained, on his first night on duty as a staff member in a large parish, he answered a desperate telephone call from a woman who had just learned that her sister had died in a plane crash. Although she wasn't at all sure—especially now—that she believed in God, she just wanted to talk with someone." Would he come?

Pastor Albacete assured her that he would come. He explains how the pastoral visit unfolded: "I brought some doughnuts and coffee with me. I wasn't there to discuss theology, to propose intellectual answers to the questioning in her heart. I told her that although I believed that her sister had not died forever, I shared the demands of her grief, and we sat in her kitchen to eat the doughnuts and drink the coffee" (Albacete, 2000, p. 22).

What a definition of pastoral care: sharing the demands of a grief! Lorenzo Albacete, the new kid on the block, was Ebed-Melech to a stranger overwhelmed by her loss. I suspect that she never forgot the "rope" (his listening) or the padding (the doughnuts and coffee).

Few people want to be alone with fresh grief.

Many people have told me they remember little of a funeral sermon—but they remember the pastor coming time after time. "As busy as he was, he would just drop by to see how we were doing," one woman noted, "and he took off his coat and sat down every time. He never seemed to be in a hurry. It was as if we were his only parishioners." In that grief-stilled home, a pastor's visit was the padded rope.

In a grief-filled day that seems to have more than 24 hours, a pastor's visit or call, the padded rope, makes a difference —as does the pastor's absence.

It is not about distracting people from grief. The grief work must be done. It is rather about creatively padding the ropes. Dan Lloyd suggests, "Let the Holy Spirit care for them through you" (1997, p. 13) in the long process of adjusting to the inevitable consequences in a maze of loss. Scripture points out that Jeremiah was not "home free." In fact, he remained a prisoner. Ebed-Melech could not get him off, but he did get him out.

Pastors cannot extract people from their grief. In fact, to do so would be unpastorly. There are lessons of the soul that only bereavement can teach. But pastors can befriend grievers in their darkest despair when "I'll *never* get over this!" ricochets through the canyons of their hearts.

Rabbi Earl Grollman has spoken to thousands of grievers and trained numerous grief counselors. His conviction is certain: The best gift you offer is your presence. Your presence says, "You do not have to go through this loss alone."

Another lesson

One other lesson comes from this account. As a pastor, you do not have to do all the tugging. In fact, as Moses learned from his management consultant—his father-in-law, Jethro—a pastor cannot do all the tugging. "The work is too heavy for you; you cannot handle it alone" (Exod. 18:18), Jethro said. Ebed-Melech had 30 assistants, some, I suspect, to pull, and others to protect the pullers from interference. This topic will be explored in chapter 10.

> **Being there demonstrates that although someone has died, friends like you still remain. Being there is the most eloquent statement that you care.**
> —Earl Grollman, 1998, p. 31

Goal of Pastoral Ministry

As a pastoral caregiver, you can make a difference. The question is "Are you?"

A Spiritual Formation Exercise

1. Take a moment to read Jer. 38:1-13 aloud.
2. Pause. Ask God to speak to you through this passage.
3. Read the passage a second time. Silently. Mark any words or phrases that leap out in your reading. In your mind, imagine Ebed-Melech "comforting" Jeremiah in the process.
4. Now, from initial memory, tell the story aloud.
5. From your observation, who in your congregation is a puller? Who could, with some training and perhaps through an apprenticeship with you, become a rope-padder? God, how can I share the model of Ebed-Melech with my congregation? Through a Sunday morning sermon? a prayer meeting talk? a devotional to open a church board meeting? as the text of a funeral sermon? In what ways can I empower my congregation—these people you have given me to lead—to offer "padded" assistance to grievers?
6. Sing the fourth verse and the chorus of "Jesus Is All I Need."

A Story That Will Preach

It was a hot day that summer of 2000, as two young Amish men slowly rode in their buggy along Route V in southern Missouri. A Ford F-250 truck topped a hill and slammed into the buggy, killing the driver, Jonas Graber, 20, and the horse and injuring the passenger.

Someone ran to notify Graber's parents and to walk with them to the scene of the accident.

The parents knelt beside their son's mangled body, kissed him, and said good-bye.

People at the scene were speechless. One said, "If that had been my boy, I would have been hysterical." The parents were informed that the driver of the truck had not been speeding but that he would be cited for "careless and imprudent driving." He had been distracted by farm equipment and had not seen the slow-moving buggy.

Meanwhile, the driver sat sobbing in the backseat of a police car. The father walked over to the cruiser and spoke softly to the man. In an action that stunned onlookers and police, he stretched out his hand to the man. A brokenhearted father and a devastated driver shook hands.

One witness said, "I have never seen anything like that in all my life" (Kavanaugh, 2000, p. A5).

I doubt anyone had ever seen anything like a eunuch heading up a committee to lift a prophet out of a cistern either.

Bereavement offers us moments to make a difference. One action may lead someone to say, "I have never seen anything like that in all my life."

A Leadership Decision

As a result of reading this chapter, I want to do the following:

1. _____

2. _____

Leadership is not about avoiding risk. Leadership is about *taking* risks.

3

Moving Beyond "Stage" Thinking

Kubler-Ross was an early leader and an important publicist for efforts to understand coping with dying. Although we all benefitted from the work of Kubler-Ross, we cannot simply lean upon her work for the rest of time. . . . [Pastors must] go beyond the inadequacies of the stage-based model.
—Charles A. Coor, 1993, p. 81

Key Point Summary
Traditionally pastors have relied on some variation of Kubler-Ross's "stages of grief" to counsel and support grievers. Pastor-leaders, however, recognize that the system is too simplistic and may, in fact, harm grievers by implying that grief is a linear process to be finished rather than a cyclical process to be experienced.

People of faith commonly respond to the bereaving through a "shorthand" of clichés (Steinsaltz, 1999, p. 187), easy answers, and the "stages of grief." Some take the stages of grief literally.

The dominant model: The five stages of grief

Many clergy and pastoral care professionals can flawlessly recite the stages of grief:

anger ➤ denial ➤ bargaining ➤ acceptance ➤ growth

Kubler-Ross's sequence has been the dominant model since its introduction in the 1960s.

J. William Worden comments, "After her first book, *On Death and Dy-*

ing (1969), many people expected dying patients [and the bereaving] literally to go through the stages she had listed in some neat order" (1991, p. 35). This model is the only resource taught in many graduate programs in medicine and nursing (Downe-Wambolt and Tamlyn, 1997; Coolican, Stark, Doka, and Corr, 1994) as well as numerous clinical psychology and graduate theology programs. Kubler-Ross is the only model many pastors know.

The original focus

The original Kubler-Ross research was not on bereavement, but rather on awareness of impending death. The notion of stages spread like wildfire because of its "immediate attractiveness" (Corr, Nabe, and Corr, 1997, p. 152) to busy clinicians and pastors.

Soon the stages of grief were applied to the divorced, the downsized, pastors being voted out of churches, and so on. You name the loss, and it could be overcome by doing the stages properly! Kubler-Ross might as well have carved this in granite: *Anyone* experiencing loss has to go through the five stages. Two goals were always clear: "Get over it" and "Move on."

Giving credit where credit is due

Kubler-Ross in 1969 alerted clergy and mental health caregivers to three realities:

- People who cope with grief often need to address some unfinished business before they can deal with the death.
- Pastors cannot effectively offer care without deliberately listening to the bereaving to help identify their needs.
- Pastors need to learn from grievers so they can know themselves better and care for their flock more effectively (Corr, 1993, p. 75).

The limitations of the theory

Corr, Doka, and Kastenbaum (1999), after an extensive review of the social science research literature, concede that Kubler-Ross was a response to dehumanizing technology in medical care. Soon, however, the patient referred to as "the cancer case" became "the angry one" or "the one in denial," and a new categorization system was in place.

All theories exist within a set of boundaries. Practitioners must be cautious in borrowing ideas and then extrapolating them to other environments without serious reflection. Otherwise you end up with sweeping generalizations such as "All grievers go through the five stages." While many do experience denial or anger or bargaining, not all do.

The uniqueness of a thumbprint

I demonstrate the inadequacy of stages by asking grievers to examine their thumbs. Then I explain, "No one has the same thumbprint as you.

Out of 6 billion humans on earth, you are unique. Now, if your thumbprint is unique, why wouldn't your 'grief print' be unique as well?"

While bereavement is a universal phenomenon, individuals experience grief uniquely and particularly. While tens of thousands will have sons die, this particular parent sitting in front of you lost a particular son with whom they had a particular relationship similar to but different from the relationship with other children. This particular grief must be recognized, examined, and honored.

> **Kastenbaum's objections to continued use of the Kubler-Ross model.**
> - **The existence of these stages has not been demonstrated by empirical research.**
> - **No evidence demonstrates that grievers actually move from anger to growth in a clear linear progression.**
> - **The limitations of the methods that led to the development of the theory have not been acknowledged.**
> - **The totality of a person's life, for example, previous losses, is neglected in favor of the supposed stages.**
> - **Resources, pressures, and characteristics of the immediate environment, which cannot be ignored, are not considered.**
> —Robert Kastenbaum, as cited in Corr, 1993, p. 70

Thomas R. Golden, after extensive work with male grievers, finds what are commonly described as "stages" are really experiences that have no particular order. Thus, when the stage progression is held up as a litmus test with which all grievers are to audit their experiences, rather than being helpful, comparison interferes with thorough grief (cited in Brooks, 1999, p. 46).

The pastor was once the primary grief counselor in the community. Grief was a spiritual issue. Now, however, that responsibility (and opportunity) is shared with funeral directors, aftercare counselors, psychologists, social workers, counselors, and physicians.

Unfortunately, Kubler-Ross has become a "one size fits all" guideline for busy pastors interacting with grieving parishioners.

Going beyond Kubler-Ross

In rejecting Kubler-Ross, some clinicians have created replacement theories. A few have outstaged Kubler-Ross. (At one hospice conference, participants were offered a 16-staged, color-coded system.) Still, the common denominator in stage-centered theories is the contention that by moving through a series of stages or phases of adjustment, grievers achieve some form of "recovery" from the death. This recovery may be commonly verbalized as "getting over it" or "getting on with life" rather than *reconciliation with* or *integration of* the death (Neimeyer, 1998). Jennifer Mirabella contends that grievers do not recover but rather "deal with, cope with, and grow" because of what they experience. The term *recovery* "is based on a medical model resulting in the eradication of symptoms" (2000, p. 22).

Stage theory enthusiasts—especially laypersons—assume that *everyone* must complete the stages in something of a linear, orderly, and predictable fashion. Grievers are forced into "a pre-established framework that reduces their individuality to little more than an instance of one of five categories (anger, or depression, or . . .) in a schematic process" (Corr, Nabe, and Corr, 1997, p. 154).

> **The identification of stages as the "normal" grief pattern infringes on an individual's freedom to grieve uniquely and thoroughly.**

The problem may be semantics

If pastors and laity said, "*Many* people grieve in the following manner," there would be less of a problem. But somewhere, lurking in the minds of the helper and the griever, "many" becomes "all," and another word gets attached: *should*. Thus, what is a suggested process in the arsenal of some pastors becomes obligatory or prescriptive.

> **No one has to [grieve] in any particular way. To insist that individuals must cope . . . in what others regard as the "right" or "correct" way is simply to impose the additional burdens of an external agenda upon vulnerable persons.**
>
> **—Charles Corr, 1993, pp. 73-74**

I often wonder what many pastors who are "stage-ists" would have done with the prolonged emotions of one of the most dramatic grievers in the Bible: Joseph. When Jacob died, "Joseph threw himself upon his father and wept over him and kissed him" (Gen. 50:1)—unmanly! The family and others grieved for 70 days (v. 3)—excessive! Then Joseph and his brothers traveled out to Atad for the committal, where they "lamented loudly and bitterly" (v. 10). Moreover, "Joseph observed a seven-day period of mourning for his father" (v. 10)—troubling!

Rethinking stage thinking

In a busy world, many grievers assume clergy to be grief experts and to have had extensive training in grief. It's not uncommon for a griever to say in a very pragmatic world, "Just tell me what I need to do." What often goes unsaid is "to get over *this* loss and get on with life" or "back to normal." Little surprise that some clergy condense compassionate grief care down to just five stages to remember: anger, denial, bargaining, acceptance, and growth. "Do the stages—you'll be fine."

In reality, they will never get back to the old normal. In time, with pastoral support, they will discover a *new* normal.

Objections to the Stages Approach

Objection 1: It reduces the mystery

Stage thinking reduces the mystery of death to a quantitative experience. Grievers are encouraged to stay busy and get over the death rather than fully embrace and experience the journey to reconciliation with the loss.

For many, grief becomes something of a prison sentence to be served, with time off for good behavior.

Previous generations of pastoral care givers would be distressed over our rush to get over grief. Until recent times, grievers experienced no time pressure or haste to get over a loss.

England's Queen Victoria grieved the rest of her life after Prince Albert's death, and her pattern became a standard of grief. "Take as long as you need" became common pastoral guidance.

I think the Matthew text can be paraphrased, "Blessed are those who drain the cup of mourning." Jesus asked His disciples, "Are you able to drink of this cup?" (see Matt. 20:22). "Sure," they responded. Today rather than draining the cup, most people want only a sip.

When someone comes with a fresh grief experience, that griever is not coming to a clinical psychologist, but to a pastor—one anointed and *called* to comfort. You are the shepherd.

The clinician allocates time to grievers in blocks, generally in exchange for money, that is, the 50-minute hour. "Time's up. See you next week." Not so with the pastor-leader.

Objection 2: It's linear rather than bidirectional or cyclical

Many interpret the stages and conclude that grief is like a checklist: "Let's see—I've the denial and the anger. Now on to the bargaining." For some, stage thinking resembles elementary school: second grade (anger) follows first grade (denial); third grade (bargaining) follows second grade, and so on. Keep making progress, and soon you'll graduate.

Objection 3: It emphasizes surviving rather than experiencing

As generally taught, stages theory is focused on a desired result: getting over this death.

Stage-embracing pastors would have difficulty hearing out the experienced grief of former United States President Dwight Eisenhower, as described a few pages back. A quarter century after the death of his son, Icky, he wrote another grieving father not to expect to ever get over it. Geoffrey Perrett observed that, four decades after the death, the leader of the free world "had never stopped grieving over Icky, and never would" (1999, p. 350).

Imagine a minister counseling the president, "Come on, Ike—you've got to get over this!"

Objection 4: It creates a false sense of security

In seminars with clergy and graduate students in ministry, whenever I question, let alone discount, the Kubler-Ross mantra, the emotional distress has been immediate, from shock to outrage. One pastor insisted, "But Kubler-Ross *has* to be true!" Another snapped, "You've destroyed everything I've ever taught about grief in my ministry!"

Objection 5: It is scientifically questionable

Grief is a detour in what Soong-Chan Rah calls our "rush on by" society. Simply put, professionals bought into the teaching of Kubler-Ross despite reservations, because the theory could be easily communicated. Now a sizable group of scholars and clinicians dismiss the underlying foundation of stages theory (Feigenberg, 1980; Kastenbaum, 1998; Pattison, 1977; Shneidman, 1980/1995; and Weisman, 1972/1977). Charles Corr, a leading grief educator, summarizes the doubts: "More than 20 years later there is still no confirmation of its validity or reliability. In fact, some of the most knowledgeable and sophisticated clinicians who work with those who are coping with dying have made clear their view that the stage-based model put forth by Kubler-Ross is inadequate, superficial, and misleading" (1993, p. 70).

> **It is not how to find an answer, but how to live without one.**
> **—Mother whose son died on Pan Am Flight 103**
> **Cited in Worden, 1991, p. 16**

Corr, Doka, and Kastenbaum caution that professional caregivers can subtly, even if unintentionally, pressure individuals into accepting stage thinking. Some pastors hint, "Don't disappoint me." Others resort to an overblown sense of power and authority. Any theory, even those advanced in following chapters, must be used as a guide rather than being imposed on a griever.

Objection 6: It reduces the freedom to grieve thoroughly

If the stages approach is assumed to be *the* right way to grieve, the grief of those who deviate from the norm is too easily labeled abnormal or pathological. The suggestion comes, "Perhaps you need to see someone" (such as a psychologist) in order to get over this death or "take something" (such as an antidepressant). Today it is becoming easier to refer a grieving parishioner to a Christian counselor rather than to "'hear another's pain'" (Parachin, 2000, p. 16).

Objection 7: It focuses on emotional responses rather than behavior and meaning-making

Grievers may suppress real feelings or questions so as not to disappoint those they consider spiritual authorities. In some cases a pastoral encounter may have been prompted by a family member seeking to enlist the pastor's or chaplain's intervention: "Could you talk to Jan? Maybe she'll listen to you." It's tempting for any busy pastor who's quick to say, "I'm not a counselor," to dispense

> **Pastor-leaders take moments to express compassion and to say, "Don't be afraid to become who you are: a griever!"**
> **—Joe Nassal, personal correspondence**

the five stages of grief in a "Listen up so I don't have to repeat this" manner rather than to listen to the end of a griever's sentences. Just as some physicians instantly grab a prescription pad, "Here—take this three times a day," so some pastors make the stages progression a spiritual prescription for grief relief.

Objection 8: It focuses on the chief mourner rather than on the significant others impacted by the death

Robert A. Neimeyer argues that "loss can only be understood in a broader social context" (1998, p. 97). Think of this as three overlapping rings: self, family, and broader society, including the church family. However, as Sandy Sheehy establishes, church friends are often treated as "secondary mourners."

> Funerals remain a family affair, coordinated by and designed to comfort spouses, daughters, sons, and siblings and their children. . . . A granddaughter who has seen the deceased no more than a handful of times in the past decade is expected to cry and to be consoled; the close friend who was part of [the deceased's] daily life is expected to bring a pie or casserole to help feed the assembled family and to offer them that consolation *(2000, p. 251).*

Like the pebble tossed into a pond, a death touches a lot of emotional shoreline.

Stage theorists, by focusing exclusively on the chief mourner, overlook the friends, the social networks, and communities of faith in which the loved one lived. Church friends, for example, are expected to put their grief for the deceased "on the back burner" in order to "be there" for family members. DelBene (1991) after years of pastoring, recognizing how wide the social shoreline may extend, routinely asks in an arrangements conference, "Tell me everyone affected by this death."

Stages as one resource in the repertoire

Stages can be *a* resource in the pastor's toolbox. Problems occur if it's the *only* resource.

Unfortunately, the stages of grief will continue to be passed on in many communities of faith to that point that in some, any lapses in grief progress are considered the equivalent of "backsliding" or failure to fully trust God. Indeed, one griever was told, "Shame on you for not believing in the power of the Risen Christ" (Gilbert, 2001, in press).

Parishioners may feel that the pastor is disappointed if they do not grieve his or her way.

Alan D. Wolfelt offers words that pastors need to remember and perhaps share with grievers:

> You may have heard—indeed you may believe—that your grief journey's end will come when you resolve, or recover from, your grief. But you may also be coming to understand one of the fundamental truths of grief: Your journey will never end.

> People do not "get over" grief. My personal and professional experience tells me that a total return to "normalcy" after the death of someone loved is not possible; we are all forever changed by the experience of grief *(1997, p. 135).*

The goal for a pastor-leader is to accompany faithfully those who are "forever changed" by their experience or experiences of grief. And in Thomas Attig's assessment: to help the griever "look for some other way to love them while they are apart" (2000, p. xii). After all is said and done, grief is "a journey that teaches us how to love in a new way now that our loved one is no longer with us" (p. xviii) and, for Christians, how to love in anticipation of reunion in heaven. Thus, healthy grief is a delicate balancing act—"from loving in presence to loving in separation" (p. xviii).

How long should grief last?

The goal of stages raises the specter of timing: *How long does it take? How long will I feel this way?*

Grief takes as long as a griever needs.

Admittedly, some pastors do not have the time—or do not make it a priority of their time—to invest in grieving people, perhaps beyond an initial conversation or so, and particularly those they conclude to be "dragging this out." So they refer grievers to

- staff members who have counseling in their portfolio
- laypeople who have had a similar loss
- a church-sponsored support group or
- a professional clinician

Unfortunately, some of those psychologists and counselors also cling to some residue of Kubler-Ross or to some modified spinoff.

Never underestimate parishioners

Some grieving parishioners through their own reading or experience with previous losses are aware of the inadequacies of the Kubler-Ross model. If you as a pastor offer only the five stages of grief, rather than listening to the being-lived-out experience of the griever, your influence will be limited.

We do not help grievers by offering easy answers based on "the stages of grief." Les Parrott III concedes that rebuilding one's life after a significant loss is hard work and "necessitates a great deal of grace on the part of the counselor" (1999, p. 335). It also necessitates an abundance of grace on the part of the pastor, as well as, I would add, caring friends and a community of faith. As a result of commitment to companion grievers, pastor-leaders become very familiar with "the valley of the shadow of death."

What if a colleague relies on stage thinking?

In some religious communities an unquestioned reliance on "the preacher says so" still exists. While you and your parishioners may not function in such a system, family members in other congregations may. As a pastor-leader, you may be called upon to break a family grief "logjam" created by a family member's reliance on what "Brother So-and-So says" about grief. This always requires diplomacy and tact. What will you do with the debunking of this popular theory?

- Give this chapter some serious reflection, perhaps another reading.
- Avoid the temptation to become a zealous crusader determined to "stamp out" the last vestiges of Kubler-Ross theory in your community of faith.
- Deal graciously with the grieving parishioner who knows only Kubler-Ross. One characteristic of a good shepherd, in the Isaiah imagery, is the ability to gently lead (see Isa. 40:11).

A pastoral response

Pastors must give serious reflection to pastoral care in a post-Kubler-

Ross era. As a pastor-leader, you can stretch the understanding of your congregation through some of these ways:
- an article in your church newsletter
- consultation with church staff—pastoral, lay, and clerical
- comments in funeral sermons
- counseling individuals and families
- training those who conduct bereavement ministry in the life of the congregation
- a sermon to the congregation or sharing through other teaching opportunities
- a special seminar or workshop

The pastor does not have to publicly debunk stages thinking, but he or she can acquaint the congregation with other ways of experiencing grief and enfranchising grievers to experience thorough grief.

Farewell

The stages-of-grief model is well entrenched and will be difficult to dismantle. Some readers may at this moment be uncomfortable with this dismissing of stages. But ministry in this era requires fresh ideas and new insights. It's time to say farewell to the stages-of-grief model so that we can embrace ideas that translate more readily into the lives of grievers today.

Goal of Pastoral Leadership

The pastor-leader seeks to facilitate and support the griever through recognition that grief is a highly individualistic process that does not always follow clear paths and sequences. Rather, every grief has right turns, left turns, U-turns, and dead ends. And when these occur, the pastor-leader is present to offer care.

A Spiritual Formation Exercise

1. Take a moment to read Luke 7:11-17, Jesus' encounter with a funeral procession of a young man, possibly an adolescent.
2. Read the passage a second time slowly. Let your finger follow the text.
3. Pause. Ask God to speak to you through this encounter with scripture.
4. Close your eyes and "watch" the incident in the life of Jesus and a young man unfold. Notice the people, possibly a large number of teen friends of the dead young man, in the "large crowd" (v. 13). How are they expressing grief? What does their body language say about their grief? What do they say when Jesus stops the procession?
5. Spend some time with this phrase: "and Jesus gave him back to his mother" (v. 15).

6. Ask, "How can we give back a deceased loved one to an adolescent?"
7. Pray, *Lord, what do You want to say to me through this reading?*

A Story That Will Preach

Once upon a time a great king owned a beautiful diamond. But there was a problem.

The diamond had a flaw--a scratch in the middle. It could never be given, worn, or admired.

So the king, who was used to having his subjects make him happy, sent word throughout his vast kingdom that great riches, position, and prestige would come to any individual who could take away the flaw. They came, the best of the jewelers and artists, even magicians—not just from that kingdom, but from across the mountains and the seas. But alas—no one could remove the scratch. The king despaired.

Then one day a young man arrived, somewhat optimistic about his chances for doing what no one else had been able to do. Oh, he heard the doubters and the scoffers. But he asked for a quiet place to work where he would not be disturbed.

Every day the king asked, "Well?" and the determined young man would answer, "Not yet."

Days passed. Weeks passed. Then one afternoon the young man handed the diamond to the king. Slowly a smile spread cross the king's face, and then a great "Yes!" ricocheted through the palace. The queen, the courtesans, and the knights crowded in for a closer look.

The scratch was still there! But the young man had carved a rose around it, using the scratch for a stem (adapted from Brener, 1993, pp. 231-32).

A Leadership Decision

As a result of reading this chapter, I need to remember:

1. _____

2. _____

> Each of us grieves at our own temple, in our own way. There is no proper way to grieve. Some of us do it by storms of tears, some by mountains of work, some by paralyzing inertia. Some flail in it like a raging river. Some cross it like a trackless waste. It can be oceanic, heaving the bereft survivor like great waves that rise, then pass. It can be fine and subtle as the late autumn air, tinged with smoke and ashes. Grief is many things, but above all it is personal. It is normal.
>
> —Julia Cameron, 2000, pp. 207-8

4

Ministering in a "Grief-Lite" Culture

The reason you were called to lead a remnant of God's people is not because of your potential to change the world (only God, Himself, can do that) but because of your availability to be used as a living instrument of His grace, power and wisdom.
—George Barna, 1993, p. 164

Key Point Summary

Pastor-leaders do not minister in a vacuum. Pastor-leaders offer care to a particular individual in a particular family in a particular congregation in a particular community at a particular time in a particular culture. That's why the pastor-leader seeks God's anointing every time.

Grief care is as an act of mercy and hospitality. Paul instructed the believers at Rome, "Share with God's people who are in need. Practice hospitality" (Rom. 12:13). Historically, burying the dead and comforting the bereaving were considered acts of mercy and "brotherly kindness" (Basilos, 1991, p. 425). But offering servanthood in grief care today is more challenging than even a generation ago as the pastor-leader navigates a minefield of cultural change. Nevertheless, "To be a New Testament church the emotional healing of people must be taken into account" (Galloway, 2000) in light of social trends.

According to cemetery consultant Donald Potter, "It doesn't matter how well you did things in the past, because the past is just that: it's past" (2000, p. 21).

Pastoral leadership takes place in a culture reassessing and restructuring the role of the pastor

Marshall Shelley captures the changes in the role of a pastor by comparing change to a stream. What began as "pastor" (from the Latin for "shepherd") evolved into "preacher" during the early Reformation. The Puritans in the 1600s used the phrase "physician of the soul" or "curer of souls" (from which the word *curate* emerged). John Wesley in the 1700s saw the pastor as preacher *and* overseer of small groups that nurtured believers (Shelley labels this "the arranger of relationships"). Simply, "The task of protecting and feeding the flock has widened" (Shelley, 2000, p. 34). Now pastors find themselves as managers, overseeing the operations of a church. Adam Hamilton identifies the pastor as a chief executive officer (CEO): "The pastor of the large church has much in common with entrepreneurial CEO's of small and mid-size companies" (2000, p. 15), which means, "As senior pastor of a large church, you no longer do the 'hands-on' work you once did. Staff does this."

The new paradigm in leadership:
You do not do—you supervise those who do.

Hamilton admits that in his congregation he conducts less than half of the funerals because not only is he CEO but also spiritual leader, preacher, head coach, visionary, and fund-raiser.

Although not every reader leads a megachurch, increasingly the large church pastors are seen as role models for pastoring in contemporary society. Their style is adopted by pastors of medium-size, even smaller, congregations. Audrey Harris and Cynthia D. Weems, who pastor small churches, respond to the ongoing restructuring by pointing to the place for the small church.

"As pastors in small membership churches, [we find that] our ministries are also shaped by our presence among the people of the church and community" (Harris and Weems, 2000, p. 9). Moreover, "Members of small churches often highly value the presence of their pastor as a community member and see this presence as a symbol of their commitment to a shared ministry" (p. 9). Conflict arises when the pastor has one model of presence in mind and the members of the church embrace another.

Whether in the church of 100, 500, or 1,000, the pastor-leader serves actively as God's ambassador in the valley of the shadow of death.

But just as ambassadors have staff to assist them, so do pastor-leaders. In fact, Galloway contends, "If I try to do all the pastoral care for the grieving, I am robbing people who have care gifts. I am helping them discover and develop gifts which bring them joy" (Galloway, 2000). The size of the congregation does impact participation in ministry. In some, the pastor assumes, "If it's to be, it's up to me!" When there are fewer participants in a setting than are needed for optimal functioning and support, people are coerced into participation. "Smaller settings thus have a higher proportion of people participating and filling roles they would otherwise leave to specialists" (p. 118). Nevertheless, words like the following from Adam Hamilton seem very tempting to pastors who do not have staff or trained volunteers: "Your task is not to do all of the pastoral care. . . . Instead, you are to insure that the systems are in place so that excellent pastoral care is delivered by someone to everyone that is in need" (2000, p. 15).

> The pastoral caregiver, then, is ideally suited to recognize the significance of a person's spiritual experience for bereavement adjustment specifically, as well as for mental and physical health generally, and to address this often under-utilized dimension of a person's experiences in promoting a griever's personal recovery following the death of a loved one.
> —Easterling, Gamino, Sewell, and Stirman, 2000, p. 274

The risk in this therapeutic era is that grievers see pastors as free grief counselors. But the pastor never forgets that he or she is present in this grief as a spiritual leader. Grief offers a "moment of opportunity for aiding the bereft in further developing or accessing their internal spiritual resources" (Easterling, Gamino, Sewell, and Stirman, 2000, p. 274). What is needed is pastors who clearly see their role as spiritual guides rather than ad hoc therapists.

Care takes place in nomadic, transitional-lite communities

"Here today, gone tomorrow" translates, "In this community of faith today but in another tomorrow." Americans are spiritual migrants. People once spent an entire lifetime—or a significant portion of a lifetime—in a particular spiritual community, or at least a denomination.

Today congregations, especially growing independent congregations, are fluid. You have a person this Sunday, but will you have him or her next Sunday? According to Dale Galloway, dean of the Beeson Center at Asbury Theological Seminary, people who leave the congregation are one of the two greatest "pain points" for contemporary pastors. "It's like a continual bleed. There's no closure when they drop out, often without explanation" (Galloway, 2000). The loss of key members to death, together with the loss of people through relocation or finding another church, can be soul-draining.

Consider these observations:
- One in five American households (17.8 million) will move this

year—whether down the street, across the state or country, or, in the emerging global economy, across the world. (USA is a mobile nation, December 6, 2000, p. 1A).

- Some, after arriving in the new place, conclude, "Why bother to put down roots? Who knows how long we'll be here?"
- "Neighbor" and "friend" are not necessarily synonymous.

Americans also trade for the next rung on the career ladder or to hang on to a job. Who in a current community is empowered to offer support? Who even knows the griever(s) well enough to offer support? Who will show up at their front door with casseroles and ask, "How can I help?" This is a growing issue for the "snow bird" retirees who may be hundreds or thousands of miles from a primary support network when a loved one dies.

> **Americans trade friends, familiarity, and a larger yard for a bigger house, a better salary, and the opportunities afforded by a larger city.**
> —N. Walfoort, November 27, 1998, p. A5

Pastoral leaders realize that today's congregation is a fluid organization

Pastors once knew their flock well. Today pastor-leaders bury "familiar strangers." In today's megachurches, the parishioner, by his or her own choice, or simple realities of size, may be a stranger to a pastor-leader. He or she is not involved in the circles of support, such as Sunday School classes or other small groups, that are activated in times of grief.

According to George Barna,

A number of faces in the congregation appear familiar but are hard to identify. That is partially because most churches have up to twice as many members as they have people in attendance on any given Sunday morning. An increasing cadre of young adults, too, have sidestepped the membership process altogether, failing to see its virtue, and simply come and go each Sunday without formal connections to the church. New statistics show that about one out of every seven who attends church rotates among a handful of churches *(1993, p. 45)*.

Barna adds, "The fluidity of the congregation—between this multiple church-home phenomenon and the high degree of household transience in America—makes the building of long-term, caring relationships with the congregants increasingly difficult" (p. 46). It also makes it difficult to conduct better-than-average funerals or to offer adequate support. Kenneth Chaffin, after long years as a pastor, has reassessed the role of the Sunday School class: "So much more is going on than imparting biblical facts" (2000, p. 7). Immediately after retirement he participated in a Sunday

School class, blessed with an outstanding teacher. He soon discovered, however, that the strength of the class was not the teaching but "in the community that had been created and their on going care of each other."

> They helped each other deal with the ups and downs of life-retirements, illnesses and hospitalizations, birthdays and anniversaries, the deaths of a spouse or parents. Their love and concern for each other was real and it was concretized with the giving of the time and energy to be supportive in a host of ways. And I saw this same thing happening in classes of all different age groups. What I observed could be done by any group that has learned to love each other.
> —Kenneth Chaffin, 2000, p. 7

Moreover, it is not just parishioners who are migratory; so are pastors. "Because viable churches are based upon relationship and because a strong community takes time to build, the possibility of a pastor creating a strong relational network within the congregation is minimized by short tenure" (p. 36). This can create ticklish scenarios, when a family requests that a former pastor return to conduct (or share) the funeral service.

Pastoral leaders givers must acknowledge and confront the negative corporate influence on bereavement

In a high-technological society, the corporation has power not only over work spaces but indirectly, over the private spaces of employees as well. The primary goals of efficiency, productivity, and profit mean that an individual employee cannot be left to decide how or how long to grieve following a death. Employers need a stable workforce. In many corporate settings, the griever is subtly told, "not on company time."

Large corporations need uniform personnel policies to ensure fairness in policy administration. So the employee handbook outlines bereavement leave.

"Oh, your father died. Well, let's see—that's five days off with pay. We'll expect you back at work in a week." In some businesses, however, the real expectation is communicated informally by the corporate culture. How soon did the boss come back to work after his mother died? Compassion will depend upon a supervisor's interpretation of policy and by the supervisor's experience with loss.

The new relationships

Corporate employee manuals do not always recognize new relationships within today's families, relationships that do not yet have names or terms, such as an adult son's mother's third husband. Is he a stepfather or merely her *current* husband? Suppose one of the third husband's children from a previous marriage dies. Does that qualify as family? Or what if a stepfather dies?

A Griever Named Michael

Michael's biological father deserted the family when Michael was five.

Eventually Michael's mother remarried, and her new husband treated Michael as his son but never legally adopted him. Michael had no contact until his father became ill and wanted to make amends. When he died, Michael was entitled to five days leave. However, six months later, when the man he called "Dad" died, Michael was not granted bereavement leave. Why? The company does not recognize any step-relationships.

The corporate enfranchisement of workaholicism

Americans now work longer hours than they did in previous generations. The workweek for many is far more than 40 hours. The workplace is stressful. In some industries, one has a job today but not necessarily tomorrow. In a culture that encourages grievers, "Stay busy," getting back to work as soon as possible is considered an effective remedy for grief, particularly for males. At visitations and funerals, it's not unusual to hear the question "So when will you be back to work?"

While an employer may say, "Take all the time you need," in some households, economics dictates the rush back to work—particularly with unanticipated medical and funeral expenses. Yet how can an employee not think about grief and the consequences of a death (such as the settling of an estate or the legal issues in the case of a wrongful death)?

Many people go back to work prematurely. The workplace is not al-

> At the time my son was killed in a car wreck, I was managing a high-volume fast-food restaurant. The corporate office sent a spectacular spray of flowers.
>
> At the visitation, the regional manager said, "The place isn't the same without you. So how soon can we count on you being back to work?" I went back two days after burying my 19-year-old. Two weeks later I was terminated.
>
> The regional manager informed me that my continued grief was impacting employee performance in the store.
>
> —Susan

> **When my teenaged son was killed, I was overwhelmed. I thought going back to work would get my mind off his death. The first day back, my boss walked up and slapped me on the shoulder and said, "Good to see you got all that out of your system."**
>
> **—Hector**

ways conducive to supporting the grieving. The colleagues and coworkers who sent flowers and signed a card, especially those who have never experienced a close death, may soon be uninterested in more than a "Keep it lite" discussion of the death.

"They just don't know what to say to you," one worker explains. "You have to get used to conversations that end with an abrupt, 'Well, glad to see you back.'"

Lack of experience leads to lack of perception. William F. Aaron, president of the National Funeral Director's Association, states, "The value of what death care professionals have to offer is being questioned as never

> **Today's decisions about rituals are determined by**
> - **flexibility**
> - **price**
> - **meaning**
> - **convenience**
>
> **—Mary Andres Russell, 2000, p. 20**

before" (1999, p. 4). That same generation may have little understanding of the unique role of clergy in funeral rituals. The only funeral some have experienced may have been in a movie or

on television. Increasingly, some decision-makers in a "death-lite" culture want an abbreviated grief, and possibly an abbreviated ritual. Pastors have been stunned by an attitude of "Just get 'em in the ground, padre."

Humans have an intrinsic need to ritualize and remember. Consultants are encouraging funeral directors to "educate families about how helpful these services and rituals can be" (Russell, 2000, p. 21), through presales and marketing, so the pastor has a voice to contribute to this discussion. Russell offers a question for funeral directors to use when families want direct cremation: "Would you like to have some private time for you and your family to say good-bye?" (p. 21).

The pastor-leader asks, "How would you like to say good-bye to your loved one?" or "How can I help you say meaningful good-byes?"

Admittedly, given the erosion in the standing of the pastor, or from negative experiences with clergy at previous funerals, some people distrust clergy. They may see them as little more than masters of ceremonies. What is it that clergy do that others cannot do? Besides, only tradition requires that a minister conduct a funeral.

Increasingly, many younger ministers have attended few funerals. Some are products of the thinking that children should not attend funerals and, in general, should be shielded from death. Others have attended only a few funerals but as outsiders rather than "front row-ers."

> For almost two decades, I had served as a pastor and often participated in the drama of suffering and death, but it was always happening to someone else.
> —John Claypool, 1974, p. 13

How can one effectively plan and lead liturgical drama if he or she has never been personally touched by grief? John Claypool, in his classic *Steps of a Fellow Struggler,* portrayed his "rude awakening" when a family member died.

After Claypool's daughter died, his ministry took on a whole new depth. No few pastors have started out on the wrong foot with grievers by saying, "I know what you're going through." When one unmarried pastor stated those words to a couple who had just lost an 18-year-old, the bereaving father hostilely confronted the pastor. "No, Pastor—you do *not* know! You have head knowledge. This calls for *heart* knowledge."

I have learned to respond, "Of course I don't know what you're going through. But I never will if you don't tell me what it's like."

Pastor-leaders must be alert to pharmacological influences

In segments of the medical community (and religious community), grief is perceived as a medical problem to be solved, treated, or *recovered from* rather than a psychological and spiritual experience to be explored. The offer "I can give you something to help you sleep or calm your nerves" is viewed as a compassionate response by many a physician. For those who are depressed, there is a whole range of medications to treat the problem, or, as one physician explains, "to take the edge off the grief."

Once upon a time a family doctor knew the individual and the family—a knowledge enhanced through house calls and social contact. The physician had a context in which to evaluate the patient's grief or changed circumstances. But how can a patient explain grief to a physician in the standardized less-than-seven-minute medical encounter? In the era of managed health care, few grievers have a physician who will listen all the way to the end of their sentences (Schubiner, 1991; Murphy, 1999). Moreover, death is an uncomfortable, if not taboo, topic to many physicians who are trained to *save* lives. A death is an admission of medical-technological defeat. Malpractice has tamed the ability of the physician to comfort: "If I say the wrong thing, I could get sued."

The issue becomes complicated—and life-threatening—because some people already are on multiple medications for a variety of conditions. In an age of increased care by specialists, the primary physician may not be fully aware of all the medications a griever is taking. (Moreover, a person may be using multiple pharmacies that a particular pharmacist is unaware of.) Moreover, drinking or not eating or not sleeping can also influence the drugs' effects.

> **It's not just physicians who dispense drugs. Friends or other family members may reach into their medicine cabinets or purses and pass on medications. The fact that the friend, by offering medications, is only "trying to be helpful" does not eliminate potential harm.**

In the upheaval created by grief, a person may get confused and not follow a drug regiment or, in some cases, may over- or undermedicate. The problem worsens if the deceased was the caregiver who dispensed and supervised the medications. Sometimes pastor-leaders offer care to grieving "walking zombies" who are significantly overmedicated.

Pastor-leaders must be responsive to radical changes in funeral service

The funeral service is going through rapid changes. Bill Aaron summarizes change by using the phrase "the funeral industry," a term that produces strain between funeral professionals (in Wolfelt, 2000). Edward J. Defort, editor of *The American Funeral Director*, concludes, "The funeral service profession will be playing on a completely different field in just a few short years" (2000, p. 3). Those changes will alter the playing field for pastors as well.

Once funeral directors (and pastors) dealt with clients in a "magical 5 to 10 mile radius that most operators seemed to consider

> People are busy, and searching for shortcuts, and buy products and services that help them do several things at once. Maybe that's why most combination funeral home/cemetery firms are so successful.
>
> One funeral provider in California uses a "man in the van" approach. Cremation and funeral arrangements are made in the home, the hospital, whatever location is most convenient for the family. In fact, the family is not required to visit their facility at all.
>
> —Mary Andres Russell, 2000, p. 20

'their territory'" (Potter, 2000, p. 81). These days the decision-maker may have already surfed the Net before calling the first funeral director or the pastor. Potter recommends funeral directors develop web sites that give the director "opportunity to turn the information seeker into a prospect, and with proper nurturing, into a satisfied customer" (p. 81). Churches and pastors also need web sites for the initial link to some grievers who may be across the block, across the state, or across the country.

We can expect the face of funeral service to change in just about every aspect. People and funeral service will be living in the electronic age of computerization.

While this can and will be frightening to some, the only thing certain is that the way we conduct business today will not necessarily be the way we do business tomorrow or ten years from now. The answer to the future is that we must adjust and change our business practices to meet the needs of client families *(Aaron, 1999, p. 5).*

That statement would be equally true of the delivery of pastoral care as well, especially in communities of faith that view parishioners as consumers to be won or held on to. Grievers may be expecting contact with the senior pastor; what they get is an associate. That alone can make initial contact dicey. Galloway concludes, "It's the griever's choice—if they want you, they should get you" (2000).

Increasingly funeral directors, in order to be competitive, must offer choices and options. My grandfather's best friend, Clarence Gilbaugh, was that rural community's funeral director. In my childhood, individuals knew the owner of the funeral home, the grocery store owner, the baker, the guys at the hardware store, the druggist, and the banker. You interacted with them not only in their establishments but also at the little league field and in church on Sunday. Now all of these, with the exception of the funeral home, are found under one roof at the superstore on the edge of town. And who knows, maybe in time funeral services will be offered or at least contracted there (just as insurance may be sold there in a kiosk).

In the last decade, the funeral profession has been enmeshed in the acquisition of local funeral homes and the growth of chains of funeral homes. The locally owned, locally operated (that is, family) funeral home is becoming more rare; the guys with their names on the sign may not actually own the funeral home.

While acquisitions have not resulted in "Funerals R Us" yet, large chains are influencing funeral practices far beyond their own establishments. Houston-based SCI (Service Corporation International), for example, owns over 2,800 funeral homes and 300 cemeteries; other conglomerates include Stewart and the Loewen Group, as well as smaller chains. It is estimated that the conglomerates do one-third of the funerals, particularly in large urban cores.

As a result, many independent, family-owned funeral homes are struggling to compete for or hold on to market share. They are increasingly having to rely on the wisdom of marketing consultants in order to compete and survive. Ads on obituary pages in newspapers now pit the local family-owned funeral home against the corporate out-of-state conglomerates. One ad in a small-town Florida newspaper recast the issue as "family values versus corporate profits." Consumers, particularly baby boomers, accustomed to buying everything else at deeply discounted prices, may not hesitate to comparison shop on what is considered a big-ticket expenditure. It's no surprise, then, that "casket stores" are opening in strip malls to sell caskets. As one witness testified in a suit challenging the constitutionality of a law requiring a person to be a funeral director in order to sell a casket, "I think consumers deserve the right to choose where to buy a casket, and market forces will prevail. . . . Casket retailers give consumers more choice and lower prices" (Tennessee Casket Store Law Ruled Unconstitutional, 2000, p. 8).

Market forces will also influence pastoral leadership in grief. Some pastors have noticed subtle differences in operations after a change in ownership. For pastors who have long served in a community, a corporate acquisition of a funeral home may mean changes that impact a pastor's and director's collegial relationship. The relationship may change when a "friendly" director moves on or a new director is brought in to shape up a facility. (No few managers have been terminated for not meeting quotas and producing profits.) One pastor recalls when his relationship with a funeral director friend became strained:

> Max and I had been friends for years. We had shared leadership in lots of funerals. At one point I had been his pastor. When my father died, we made the arrangements, and Max said, "We'll settle up later." Five years later, when my mother died, after making the arrangements, Max said, "John, I hate to ask this, but I need to have a $5,000 check." I looked puzzled, and he looked away for a moment. "Most people don't know this, but I no longer own this funeral home. I sold it to a group. I just manage it. My hands are tied. The policies are determined at the corporate offices. I am so sorry to have to ask this."

Thomas Lynch, a third-generation Michigan funeral director, offered this analysis of the change:

> The publicly traded, corporate enterprise is accountable to the international headquarters, the sales quota and the stockholders, while the independent is accountable to the local consumer, including very often the local loan officer.
>
> The privately owned firm cannot attribute its prices to some distant "home office" or the "district manager." It cannot blame shortfalls in service on "company policy." . . . For independents, market share—

present and future—is guaranteed by reputation, while corporates place more stock in pre-need sales. Independents count on the name on the sign; corporates count on the money in the bank *(1999, p. 94)*.

Lynch, conceding the need for preplanning, is concerned about the increased practice of preneed selling, particularly the aggressive hardball preselling.

The danger is that funerals become just like any other commodity. You get what you pay for. Little surprise that discount funeral operations are springing up around the country to challenge both the independent family-owned as well as corporate funeral homes. "Bring your own casket" (ordered off the Net) is a reality in many areas.

> The junk-mail, telemarketed, briefcase bargain of the memorial counselors and conglomerates has turned the funeral from an existential event [let alone a liturgical event] into a retail one.
> —Thomas Lynch, 1999, p. 96

Most funeral homes are managed by directors with integrity. Lynch is correct in saying that there can be "bad apples" among the independents as easily as among the chains. Unfortunately, the "bad apples" get the press. Many caring funeral directors who go the second (sometimes third and fourth) mile to make a meaningful ritual are seldom recognized for their service.

Funeral directors are in business to offer a service and to make a profit. How much service and how much profit will increasingly be issues.

What is the pastor's role in the arrangements process? Some volunteer to accompany families to the arrangements conference. Many—but not all—funeral directors welcome the pastor's presence and involvement. Does the pastor's role as shepherd stop at the casket selection room door? All sorts of family issues get dragged in to the arrangements process. Not a few families have purchased funeral goods with a "let's make it up to Dad" attitude or "Mama deserves the best." Some choices have long-term financial and relational consequences.

Another innovation is the growing number of cemeteries offering funeral services. Thus, a cemetery may become a one-stop entity (Van Beck, 1998), which also impacts competition. Indeed, more churches will develop on-site columbarium for cremated remains.

Pastor-leaders must be responsive to the growing influence of women

It was once thought "a woman's place is in the home." Now, that may be "in the *funeral* home." Indeed, women have long been active in the funeral profession, either as full partners or in behind-the-scenes roles. When I graduated from mortuary school, there was only one woman in my class of 70. Now, women make up half the students in many mortuary schools; the San Francisco School of Mortuary Science is headed by a woman. Many barriers to women offering leadership in funeral service have been eliminated. I admit—I was surprised to attend a service in which all the funeral professionals were female.

Women are more likely to be the significant leaders in planning and organizing rituals. In some families, women are the social organizers (Bern-Klug, 1999) and decision-makers. Some have a magical ability to turn the ordinary into the extraordinary. Some put aside their own grief to manage the details and look after other grievers. Once men were told to be strong; increasingly that advice is being hoisted on women. The burden for looking out for others falls heavy on a grieving woman's shoulders.

The commanding male presence of funeral directors has imposed a sense of social control, at least, over male grievers. I remember as an apprentice director being asked, "How is Ed holding up?" as if one of my jobs was to keep an eye on individual grievers. Unwittingly, funeral directors have been part of the "policing grief" (Walter, 2000, p. 1) that disenfranchises grief expression. I'm pleased by the growing involvement of women in funeral leadership, both as pastors and as funeral directors.

> **The funeral was nearly over. It was almost time to leave for the cemetery. I knew the organist was to play softly as we left the chapel. I am a stickler for everything going according to plan. But I heard something: a soft voice singing "Jesus Loves Me." Quickly I determined that the mother of the deceased child was singing. And she did not stop with verse one. Soon the funeral home was filled with that tender song. I wiped away tears as I watched her help her grief-stricken husband stand and walk to the family car. She led all the family in an unwavering voice. Earlier when I had asked her how she was holding up, she told me, "I'm taking it an hour at a time." Where does a woman find such strength?**
>
> **Not every mother sings, but more and more I am seeing women as the ones who are emotionally in-charge. Women are the strong ones. But I worry about them a month down the road when deferred grief comes calling.**
>
> **—Matt, funeral director**

Pastoral caregivers must acknowledge the growing choice of cremation

Cremation is a reality that pastor-leaders acknowledge rather than fight. Cremation is now involved in over 25 percent of all funeral arrangements. Moreover, new research indicates an increase in those who would select cremation for themselves (46 percent) or for a loved one (46 percent) with a higher percentage among highly educated and upper-income persons (Cremation Association of North America, 2000, p. 26). Historically, many conservative pastors strongly opposed cremation; some still do. But rapid social change and influence is pro-cremation. For one thing, cremation alters the time line for ritualization. Commonly, pastors hear, "This is *not* a good time for a funeral." (Is it *ever* a good time?) With no body to bury, a service no longer has to take place within the typical 72-hour time frame. Indeed, a memorial service can be postponed indefinitely or, as I read in one obituary, "until a more convenient time." Convenience is two-way. The pastor does not have to fly home from vacation or a conference; the memorial can be delayed until he or she returns.

The mobilization of family members across the landscape may mean that flying all the family members to a funeral on short notice is financially prohibitive (even with bereavement fares on the airlines). In reality, some family members attend a funeral at an enormous financial hardship.

Why People Choose Cremation

24% less expensive
17% uses less land and has less environmental considerations
7% simpler/less emotional or more convenient
11% personal preference
7% body is not put into the earth
4% cremation remains can be strewn, placed in more than one location
2% easier to ship remains to another area
2% religion
2% no reason to save the body
2% easier for the family
2% "I don't want people to see me"
2% less emotional
1% tradition in a particular family
17% other reasons and "unknown"

—Cremation Association of North America, 2000, p. 28

Many pastors assume that the leading factor in choosing cremation is cost, specifically saving money, but research does not support that conclusion. Certainly it may be a factor, but not *the* factor.

The issue becomes stressful when there is a dissension within the family over the decision to cremate or not cremate. Legally, it is the prerogative of the next-of-kin or an executor to decide, but in some families the issue is the line drawn in the sand. Sometimes, courts are being asked to intervene to prevent cremation.

A family member may seek to involve the pastor on one side or the other—sometimes without the pastor's knowledge. "Maybe they'll listen to you, Pastor." Questionable interpretation of Scripture or tradition may cloud the dialogue. A growing number of pastors prefer a bodyless memorial service—cremation removes the body.

Traditionally, many funeral directors have opposed cremation as well. However, the National Funeral Directors Association has worked tirelessly to help directors see cremation as an option they can offer clients. Families may even schedule a limited visitation. Or they may ask the director to embalm, then cremate after a visitation or a funeral service. The family rents a casket with a disposable liner.

Pastors should be concerned by a statistic supplied by the Cremation Association of North America: in 1996, 233,000 cremations (or 47 percent of the total) involved *no* services (Russell, 2000, p. 20).

Pastor-leaders acknowledge multiculturalism

Diversity is a key ingredient in making funeral arrangements. Diversity even shapes liturgy for rituals, particularly in metro urban areas. Issues about diversity can be heightened when it comes to determining funeral plans, especially if the deceased dies without a will or expressed ritual wishes. "Can't we all get along, at least until we can get him [her] in the ground?" is no longer an uncommon expression.

Many growing churches are racially mixed. Individuals bring cultural traditions with them to a formerly predominately white church. Intermarriage may lead to a request to bury a church member or a distant member of their family. There can be enormous pressure when members, in their commitment to Christ, reject a family or faith tradition's rituals. I have worked with Hispanic Evangelicals who angered their families by not attending a rosary service. That resentment may remain an issue long after the funeral. Others, for example, face similar issues with the celebration of Días de los Muertos, Days of the Dead, in November. With a growing Hispanic population, even in rural areas, pastor-leaders will have to learn more of this tradition.

Needless to say, diversity is an issue for a pastor and a congregation when arranging rituals for gays and lesbians. The pastor must be sensitive not only to the family of origin but also to the family of choice—particularly a partner. One pastor recalls his experience:

> I thought that will never happen here in my small town. But I got the call, "Pastor, our son is dead and we would like you to do the funeral." I had never met him, but I knew the tensions that had existed in the family. All I could think of were the words of that old song, "Lord, lay some soul upon my heart / And love that soul through me." I had sung it, but I wasn't sure I could live it. The young partner didn't have a pastor or much of an appreciation of pastors. But I knew that Jesus wanted me to reach out to him in his sorrow. Some family members were pretty ugly to that young man and to me. It's one thing to wear the WWJD bracelet: What would Jesus do? It's something else to do it in a small town. If nothing else, I wanted to change the stereotype of pastors as hell-breathers to those gay friends who filled that funeral chapel that day. I guess I had two congregations in one funeral. I did my best.
>
> But I was really pleased with my people. We always provide a meal for the family and out-of-town quests. And I just said, "This is something we need to do." My people rolled out the hospitality.

The pastor-leader draws few lines in the sand, but when he or she does, everyone clearly sees the rationale for his or her decision.

Conclusion

The pastor faces a challenge of redefining pastoral leadership in light of change in this culture. Some pastors find great comfort in doing grief work "by the book" with no deviations. It is far easier to pour the ritual into a form: a verse of Scripture followed by a poem and a prayer rather than to be innovative—or to sit there wondering, "Is this [innovation] going to work?"

Pastor-leaders do not cling to what has worked in the past.
Pastor-leaders hear freedom in the hymn's words
"To serve the present age, my calling to fulfill."

It may have been easier on pastors and funeral directors in the "good old days" of ritual predictability, but in reality, today is tomorrow's good old day. The line of Charles Wesley's text cautions pastors, "O may it all my pow'rs engage / To do my master's will!" In reality, conducting a good funeral is part of the Master's will, despite the significant cultural shifting. Pastor-leaders are called to partner with change. I suspect that good pastors many years ago fought the "innovation" of visitations and funerals held in funeral homes, preferring the historic tradition of in-home visitations and in-church funerals. But change happened without them.

> Who knows but that you have come
> to royal position for such a time as this?
> —Mordecai to Esther, Esther 4:14

Pastor-leaders know that they may be able to win a skirmish, but they look ahead to continuing to be a pastoral presence in the griever's life. The question "Is this issue worth losing the potential for future ministry over?" is always in the pastor's thinking.

Goal of Pastoral Leadership

The pastor-leader is expected to balance sensitivity to the needs of the family and sensitivity to cultural change and shift. The pastor-leader seeks to lead mourners in an unrepeatable opportunity for spiritual engagement and reflection with the reality of death. The pastor-leader works to build bridges for future interaction.

A Spiritual Formation Exercise

1. Take a moment to read Ps. 137.
2. Slowly read the passage aloud. This psalm is written by an individual grieving the loss of the familiar. What in the psalm text demonstrates that?
3. Read verse 1 with as much emotional intensity as you can muster. What words in the verse leaped out at you?
4. Read verse 4. Now read, "How can we sing the songs of our Lord while *in a land called grief?*" How would you answer a griever who poses this question? In poetic form answer the following question: How can we sing the Lord's song in a land called grief?

   _____
   _____
   _____
   _____
   _____
   _____

5. In what ways in funerals past have you sung "the Lord's song" in a strange place? Now think of a recent funeral. List the names of people who, as a result of this death, are asking, "How do we sing the Lord's song in this strange land?" Take a moment to hold each person up to the Lord.
6. Begin with this prayer fragment: *Lord, as I read about these changes that affect the way I offer ministry, I feel . . .*
7. Sing these words of Charles Wesley: "To serve the present age, /

My calling to fulfill; / O may it all my pow'rs engage / To do my Master's will!"
8. Pray, *God, please equip me to serve this present age.*

A Story That Will Preach

David Whyte spins an intriguing story about hiking with a group in the Himalayas. Studying the maps, he decided to do a three-day trek on his own. He would meet up with the team at a certain bridge for the last of the adventure. So for three days he had had an experience of a lifetime—man against nature—as he walked slowly toward the bridge. But when he arrived, he was stunned. The chains that held the bridge were in disrepair; moreover, many of the boards were missing. The rickety bridge was hanging perilously 400 feet in the air. Dared he risk trying to cross?

After studying his maps, he realized that there were no close alternative routes around the gorge. It was either this bridge—and the very real possibility of death—or retrace his three-day path and miss rendezvousing with the team.

As he was groaning with indecision, an elderly mountain woman walked into the clearing carrying a heavy sack. She had been collecting the dried dung she would use to build fires in her home. She greeted the traveler with the simple word *"Nimaste,"* the Indian equivalent of "Hello." Without waiting his acknowledgment, she walked across the bridge to the other side. He jumped up and without hesitation followed her across.

Sometimes a griever needs someone to lead the way across the dangling bridge called bereavement. As a pastor-leader, you could be as empowering as the lady carrying the basket.

A Leadership Decision

As a result of reading this chapter, I need to

1. _____

2. _____

Many Christians have a rather selective recitation of the words of James 1:27. He only cautions us to "keep oneself from being polluted by the world" (1:27), not from being aware of the world around us. But more sobering words are found in Ezekiel: "I will hold the watchman accountable" (33:6).

5

Leading in the Era of Church Growth

It is a rare and distinctive privilege of ministry to be welcomed into the small, quiet, broken circle of the family in such critical times.
—Thomas Oden, 1983, p. 294

Key Point Summary

Ministry with the dying and the bereaving must never be routine or "by the book" or taken for granted or be considered simply one more thing to squeeze into an already busy day. Grief leadership is Kingdom work.

Increasingly, ministers struggle to begin to meet the demands of a modern church, particularly the growing parish. Effective pastors have to hit the ground running every morning. Many pastors feel overwhelmed by their responsibilities and the informal demands of parishioners. But nothing reorders the structure and schedule like a death. How many pastors have wanted to say to a corpse, "You picked a fine time to die!"

While the standard theological curriculum and preparation for ordination requires biblical, theological, homiletical, and historical studies, in some seminaries practical theology is downplayed because of the assumption, "They can learn on the job." One small problem: You're learning on *my* family.

Rarely will a griever ask a pastor about an obscure historical incongruity of the Reformation or about a theological nuance in Tillich, Moltmann, or Wesley.

The reality is that people do not want to go to the cemetery alone. They want a pastor to remind them that God cares. They want a pastor to walk with them the path from the hearse to the tent over the hole in the ground.

In the most vulnerable moments, they want a pastor fully there with no practiced glance at a wristwatch. And in days ahead, when their grief work becomes intense, they want a pastor fully present with them.

While the ability to lead individuals in grief is not specifically included in the list of qualifications of overseers in 1 Tim. 3 or Titus 1, being "hospitable" is. Paul contends that the overseer "must also have a good reputation with outsiders" (1 Tim. 3:7). Doing a "poor" funeral or offering the grieving less-than-exemplary pastoral care is a quick way to earn a poor reputation in a family and in a community. People don't forget bad funerals. Many will not overlook or forget minimal pastoral presence with the bereaving. A pastor's initial presence will decide the extent of future interaction.

"We want to avoid any criticism of the way we administer this liberal gift" (2 Cor. 8:20). Although Paul's words specifically refer to the churches' offering for the poor, this passage has far-reaching implications for the use of ministry gifts as well, particularly in those moments ripe with potential for misunderstanding. Paul adds, "For we are taking pains to do what is right, not only in the eyes of the Lord but also in the eyes of men" (v. 21).

These words have implications for pastor-leaders: "Because of the service by which you have proved yourselves, men will praise God for the obedience that accompanies your confession of the gospel of Christ, and for your generosity in sharing with them and with everyone else" (2 Cor. 9:13). A pastor friend explained to me why he had not visited me at a single adult conference I recently led in the city where he lives. He had spent those days dealing with two single adults whose father had committed suicide in front of them. He chose to be generous in sharing the tragedy with two grieving sisters. It was an opportunity for sensitive leadership these women will long remember. My pastor friend was "taking pains."

Sensitive ministry with the bereaving cannot be learned in "Pastoral Care 101" in seminary or Bible college. Sensitivity cannot be learned from reading a book—even this book—or through a computerized distant learning experience or at a continuing education event. Sensitivity is learned in the crucible of human experience. I have been taken with Charles Gerkin's reflection on his father's pastoral presence.

> It is difficult for me to recall where and when I first experienced what I have since come to think of as care given by a pastor. . . . I do not recall my father ever using the term pastoral *care*. He was trained to offer such care only by his own experience of living and working

with the farmers and storekeepers, housewives and young people who were the members of his small congregations. He worked in the field with them, sat and talked and drank coffee with them, married their children and buried their dead. I do remember going with my father on his visits to the homes of his congregation, where as a small boy I listened as they talked about their concerns and about the ordinary things of life. When people wanted to talk about something that was deeply troubling, though I have no recollection of it, I was probably sent outside to play so that they and my father could talk more privately, intimately, and openly *(1999, p. 13)*.

> **Pastoral care is increasingly learned in the laboratory**
> **of trial and error or, as one pastor told me,**
> **"from getting your hands *and your heart* dirty."**

The funeral director is, at best, tolerated in such moments, while the pastor is, generally, welcomed. It is to the pastor that the grieving frequently turn for a "hoped-for ministry that extends through and beyond the awesome mystery of death" (Oden, 1983, p. 294). When death interrupts, the pastor has "the potential of being the most important person in the griever's life at the time" (Swift, 2000, p. 181). The pastor's care—or lack of care—will be imprinted in their memories of the loss. (One reason a pastor may not be welcomed initially is because in the last grief episode in the family a pastor was insensitive.) A pastor-leader never forgets that he or she was called and ordained for such moments, modifying Wesley's words to "assured if I their trust betray," someone will long remember that faux pas.

The minister comes bearing not answers, advice, or psychobabble on the stages of grief, but presence.

The pastor as chaplain

Some leading voices in the church growth movement dismiss the traditional pastor as a "chaplain." "The small church pastor calls on people, prays for people, cares for people, and attends every meeting as the omnipresent, always available, chaplain of the faithful" (Hunter, 2000, p. 16). For nineteen and a half centuries, that would have described an effective pastor. But no longer. Go to any church growth seminar, and the focus is this: "You have better things to do with your time than hang out with grieving people!" As one pastor informed me, "I cannot build this church and visit nursing homes. To visit a nursing home would not be a wise use of my time." It was *my* mother I wanted him to visit. Some time later, I was stunned by these words on pastoral care and grief.

"Then let them come to me, or to some other discreet and learned minister of God's words and open his grief that he may receive ghostly counsel, advice and comfort as his conscience may be relieved" (*The Book of Common Prayer*, 1552, as cited in Hatchett, 1995, p. 45).

I hasten to explain the phrase "come to me" was in the era of the small parish.

George Hunter bemoans the fact that 6 out of 10 pastors will reject this understanding of pastoring: "Many pastors and church workers like to be everybody's chaplain; they care for all their members, and they contract, counsel, and pray with people at the local barbershop, fire station, hospital, nursing home, and Moose lodge" (2000, p. 19). I suggest that one reason is that this is where they can find grievers in their flock, particularly males. And it is in these settings that individuals are more likely to acknowledge the black-and-blues of their grief. Willimon still believes in visiting parishioners: "For me, it is pastoral visitation, putting myself at the disposal of my people, that I find most ethically formative in the communal sense. I consider it essential for the task of preaching that I be present in the homes and workplaces of my people. One can learn more about someone in a living room than in years of momentary encounters at the door of the church" (2000, p. 91).

The shadow of the large church

In a culture that values the large church, many who pastor small churches are perceived as failures. There are almost 400,000 churches in the United States, and the great majority of them are small (one-half may have 75 or fewer in attendance). Leith Anderson cites Schaller's work to say that one-half of those who attend church go to the 14 percent of churches that are the largest. Anderson says that "more and more Americans are opting for 'full service churches' that can offer quality and variety in music, extensive youth programs, diverse educational ministries, a counseling staff, support programs, etc." (1990, p. 51). *Lots of* "etc."

But I make a case that one arena in which the "full service" church cannot be as effective is in caring for the bereaving.

I admit that I have been influenced by one pastor's decision. Terry Swicegood pastored one of the largest and most prominent Presbyterian churches in the United States. "From the time I was first ordained," he admits, "I aspired to lead a large church," and in time he got his "dream" church. But some realities surprised him. He states,

> **Like it or not, large churches are a reality. They are drawing the majority of people, and big churches are getting bigger. Mega-churches of tens of thousands exert an increasingly powerful influence on everything from local politics to national religious publications.**
> **—Leith Anderson, 1990, p. 52**

The church has 3,700 members. It's impossible even over a long ministry to know 3,700 intimately. I longed for pastoral relationships, but I spent most of my time keeping the wheels of the organization greased. I was required to be astute politician, motivational speaker, discerning psychotherapist, visionary leader, and institutional fundraiser, with rarely a full day off.

The pastor in that demanding Eastern seaboard setting is like a circus juggler who runs up and down the line keeping 25 plates spinning on poles. Just as he gets a few plates spinning at one end, the plates at the far end begin to wobble. Even if he has done his best, the audience will feel that he isn't a good juggler, because he lets a plate crash *(2000, p. 27)*.

Swicegood came to believe that his people knew him through sermons, the newsletter, and persona at the church door. This was the pastorate many colleagues would give their eyeteeth for, yet it wasn't fulfilling for him.

> **"For me, one of the most important aspects of ministry is to be known, loved, and respected by the congregation as I desire to know, love, and respect them,"** he said. **"That is difficult to pull off in a crowd."**
> —Terry Swicegood, 2000, p. 27

In a stunning decision, Swicegood resigned, "without a clue as to what I was to do next." In time, he was called to pastor a church of 500 members (still large, but not a megachurch), where he writes, "I am rediscovering what it means to pastor."

"In my new church, I have the opportunity to know a few people in a deep way, rather than know many people in a shallow way. I get to teach a Bible study once a week, something I had been unable to do for years. In every death in the congregation, every birth, every illness, I am involved" (p. 27).

Does he miss it? Some things, yes, such as the music and abundant financial resources. But, he adds in words that some reader will appreciate, "My soul is at peace. I am where I need to be. I am doing the things for which I entered the ministry—listening, preaching, teaching, caring." He closes his article on his downsizing by describing an encounter with a young paralyzed male in his congregation who had developed a fascination with birdwatching. When Swicegood read an article on mockingbirds, he decided to drop it by the home (the efficient pastor would have had his secretary drop it in the mail). He writes, "We sat together for a long time--something I never could have afforded in my bustling large-church ministry—and I pondered some of the deeper mysteries of life: how the mockingbird chooses from its repertoire of 180 songs, why this young man is stricken with an awful disease, and why my ministry turned out so different than what I had expected" (p. 28).

Maybe Jesus' words could be paraphrased, "For I was grieving and you came and sat with me." Swicegood's example sounds a lot to me like Jesus' example on the Emmaus road.

WDJD: What did Jesus do?

You have seen the WWJD bracelets: "What would Jesus do?" Not a bad question for pastors to ponder before responding to a bereaving family's request, "Would you please come? We need you," not unlike the request made by Lazarus's sisters (John 11:3).

What would Jesus do in such a grief-hemorrhaging moment to communicate care and love? Perhaps strapping on a WWJD bracelet would be a great reminder to pastors walking into an emergency room, nursing home, funeral home, or residence to face individuals who have been ambushed by death's sting and whose plans, priorities, and commitments have suddenly been upended.

In many settings, upon your arrival, someone will announce, "The pastor is here," similar to words communicated to a grief-stricken Mary almost 2,000 years ago—"The Teacher is here" (John 11:28)—in what was surely a tense pastoral moment. How would you respond if the first words out of the mouth of a griever were accusatory? "If you had been here, my brother would not have died" (v. 32). Although I do not find an exclamation mark in the scripture, I am certain Jesus heard one in Martha's voice. More likely you will hear a whispered "Thank you for coming" or "It is so good of you to come at this hour." If you have taken the time to invest in people's lives, the only words they may get out are "Oh, pastor . . ."

How did Jesus respond to Mary? John discloses, "When Jesus saw her weeping, and the Jews who had come along with her also weeping, he was deeply moved in spirit and troubled" (v. 33). No routine pastoral death response. No "calm, cool, and collected" or detached, objective distancing. No "I can handle this." The moment offered Jesus an opportunity to be totally present, for His heart to take the full blast of the accusation, just as ours offer moments to be God's ambassadors in this place and space, in *this* grief. Jesus saw the chief grievers—Mary and Martha—but He also noticed the others, the friends and neighbors who were grieving as well. John comments, "He was deeply moved" (v. 33).

As a pastor, when was the last time you were "deeply moved" or "troubled"? Take a moment to explore that memory. Has death become something you deal with efficiently and effectively? Are those initial awkward moments with a family still occasions for a hurriedly whispered *O God, help me . . .* or an, "Oh, yeah—been there, done that many times. I

> People do not care how much you know until they know how much you care.
>
> —Frank Freed, Ph.D.

can handle this." "All right, now, everyone listen up. This is what Kubler-Ross calls the first stage of grief: shock!"

How does a pastor learn sensitivity in the awkward moments of life? Thomas Oden writes, "It might seem facile to answer too quickly: only by being a pastor. But that is essentially the right answer. Only by being there as the one who in other times is liturgist and preacher and teacher, but now is shepherd of souls in the presence of death. We learn what to say, in part, by listening to what is being said. If we let the person tell us where he or she is, we will soon learn how best to respond" (1983, p. 299).

How do I lead in *this* situation?

In many ways, the old patterns of clergy response seem less workable in today's society. There may well be times when a pastor concludes, "I don't know how to respond or where to begin." Lyrics by Charles Wesley have long influenced my understanding of pastoral care: "Arm me with jealous care, / As in Thy sight to live; / And O Thy servant, Lord, prepare / A strict account to give!"

"Jealous care" is, well, a little archaic. In today's vernacular it might better be translated *intentional care.* I appreciate that verse more after discovering how much time Charles Wesley spent composing lyrics for the funerals of his friends. For him, music was pastoral leadership.

Leadership has a way of making shambles of schedules, as nosily as Jesus overturned tables in the Temple.

The moment for Martin Luther King Jr. came at a committee meeting called to discuss the arrest of Rosa Parks for refusing to give up her seat on a bus. Anger and frustration set the tone until someone called on the new young preacher from Boston to say a few words. Initially, Dr. King hesitated; after all, he had just recently moved to Montgomery. But as King began to speak, a "disheartened, confused crowd began to be a movement that would in just a few years shake the world. . . . Martin Luther King that night was "ordained" to lead and thereby became a leader" (Willimon, 2000, p. 87). King later reflected on the experience:

> Little did I know when I came to Dexter that a movement would commence in Montgomery that would change the course of my life forever. But history still has its unpredictable qualities and reserves for itself elements of creative surprise. Unknowingly and unexpectedly, I was capitulated into the leadership of the Montgomery movement.
>
> Everything happened so quickly and spontaneously that I had no time to think through the implications of such leadership. I was unprepared for the symbolic role that history had trust upon me. But

there was no way out *(Martin Luther King Jr., 1959, exhibit in Hartsfield International Airport, Atlanta).*

I came to understand this more when one of my doctoral students, who had been a member of the Dexter Avenue church when Dr. King was the pastor, described the experience of a peer drowning at youth camp. I knew of Martin Luther King Jr. only as a preacher and civil rights leader. My student, though, knew Dr. King as the pastor who "worked" a front porch lined with stunned boys. The care offered that hot summer day and in the months afterward is what partially influenced my student to become a pastor. God used the loss of this pal and the example of a pastor-leader to shape the heart of a future pastor-leader.

Goal of Pastoral Ministry

Sometimes one must carefully assess the "voices" that describe success in the ministry. Sometimes one must turn down the volume on the voices that say, "Do this and you can be successful!" in order to hear the invitation of One pleading, "Feed my sheep."

A Spiritual Formation Exercise

1. Take a moment to read Luke 7:36-50, an account of lavish attention.
2. Take a deep breath. Invite God to speak to you through this encounter with Scripture.
3. Read the passage a second time. Slowly. What catches your attention? Think of a way that you have been lavish with attention for a griever.
4. Pastors always have more things on their agendas than can be done in a day. Just as Jesus was criticized, our way of expressing compassion can be a subject of criticism or challenge (v. 39). How do you respond to such criticism?
5. Spend some time with this phrase: "Then he turned toward the woman and said to Simon, 'Do you see this woman?'" (v. 44). Think about the tone of voice Jesus might have used. Now try out these words, "Do you see this griever?" in several tones of voice.
6. Ask God to show you how you see grievers.
7. Pray, *Lord, what do You want to say to me through this reading?*

A Leadership Decision

As a result of reading this chapter, I need to remember to

1. _____

2. _____

A Story That Will Preach

A preschool teacher was talking about Mary Magdalene washing the feet of Jesus when a little girl interrupted: "My mommy cries all the time." The teacher ignored the comment to refocus the attention of the class on Mary Magdalene. The little girl interrupted again: "My mommy cries all the time. My mommy cries *all* the time." The teacher again returned to the subject at hand, but the little girl was determined to be heard that day in that place.

"After my daddy died, my mommy is always crying," she explained. "I go and get in bed with her and tell her everything is all right and tell her to stop crying. But she doesn't. My mommy is always crying" (Andersen, 2000, p. 90).

That child was Caroline Kennedy; the mommy was Jackie Kennedy in those early days following the assassination of her husband, United States President John F. Kennedy, in November 1963. What if that teacher had silenced the sad child rather than recognizing this six-year-old griever needed to be listened to? Mary Magdalene's foot-washing could wait until another day. In a real sense, that day the teacher "washed" the grief of a child.

**A significant element in ministry is being
willing to be interrupted. Again.**

We must be ready to allow ourselves to be interrupted by God. God will be constantly crossing our paths and canceling our plans by sending us people with claims and petitions.
—Dietrich Bonhoeffer, 1954, p. 99

6
Reconstructing Life After Loss

We are not good about admitting grief, we Americans.
It is embarrassing. We turn away, afraid that it might happen to us.
But it is part of life, and it has to be gone through.
—Madeline L'Engle, 1988, p. 229

Key Point Summary

Pastor-leaders learn the difference between crisis interven-tion care—guiding the griever through the initial adjustment—and the longer reconstruction care. Some pastors are good at getting grievers to the middle of the stream; pastor-leaders accompany the griever through the stream and safely onto the shore.

Christians admit the facts or details of a loss, such as "My husband died on March 4," but many are reluctant to engage grief after the appropriate rituals.

In a multitude of ways, grievers are reminded that we are supposed to grieve in an orderly fashion with dual goals: to "accept God's will" and "move on."

If only there were bumper stickers that read, "Christians grieve too"!

Many grievers have strong pastoral support for the first couple of miles; after that, grievers are on their own. "See you at the finish line." In some cases it is not the death but rather the forced reconstruction of life without the loved one that requires continual pastoral attention and con-gregational support. The pastor-leader, however, shows up along the long route calling out encouragement and offering resources for the long process of reconciliation with the loss.

**The pastor-leader recognizes that grief is
more a marathon than a hundred-yard dash.**

How you handle an opportunity disguised as a crisis will go a long way in determining or undermining recognition as a spiritual leader in the community. In words still as valid as when G. B. Williamson penned them, we are reminded that funerals are a service to a church, a family, and a community: "Those that are turned to him in a natural course of events by members and friends of a church and that come providentially to him should be accepted as a sacred responsibility" (1952, p. 133). A wise pastor takes seriously this aspect of ministry and seeks to excel in both manner and message.

When some pastors hear the phrase "to comfort those who mourn" (*Manual,* 1997, par. 413.6) they hear "to bury the dead." Burying the dead is only the start of the process.

Reconstructing meaning after a loss

Robert Neimeyer, distinguished grief specialist at the University of Memphis, identifies the following "lessons of loss" grievers must master in order to reconstruct or rebuild their lives.

Lesson 1: "Grief is a personal process, one that is idiosyncratic, intimate, and inextricable from our sense of who we are" (Neimeyer, 1998, p. 89).

You are the only one who can work through your grief. An old Appalachian folksong reminds, "You've got to walk that lonesome valley; you've got to walk it by yourself . . . *nobody else can walk it for you.*" Others will cogrieve, but they did not have the particular relationship with the deceased that you had. For example, a father may have four children, but each sibling has a different relationship with him; the relationships may be similar but not identical. Because grief is so idiosyncratic, a griever can be intimidated when not grieving like other siblings. "Pastor, what's wrong with me?"

When attempts to explain collapse "and our most basic sense of self is assaulted, we lose our secure grip on familiar reality, and we are forced to reestablish another" (Neimeyer, 1998, pp. 89-90). Attempts to explain often fall on "confused" ears and hearts. A platitude creates enormous anger that may go unverbalized but nevertheless is spiritually destructive. Easy "listen up" answers by a pastor threaten credibility for future conversations.

> I'm ninety-four. What good am I to anybody? Why did the Lord take my grandson and leave me here? I wish someone would explain this to me. He had his whole life ahead of him.
>
> —Mildred, participant in a Grief Gathering

How is leadership viewed in such moments? The family, as well as observers, will long cherish clear leadership, which sometimes may be "outside the lines" of tradition.

Pastors who lead grievers who are asking, "Who am I *now?*" are valued. This may be the case when a parent loses an only child, especially if a single parent. Who am I without my child?—or in cases of particular need, without *this* child (regardless of the child's age)? Or when the chronically ill person loses his or her caregiver to a heart attack. Pastors also ask the question when the deceased was a strong supporter.

Consider the assault on the worldview of Jackie Kennedy by the president's assassination (she had already suffered a miscarriage, a stillbirth, the death of a father, and the death of a son, Patrick).

After her brother-in-law Robert Kennedy was assassinated in 1968, Mrs. Kennedy concluded, "If they are killing Kennedys, my children are the number-one targets. I want to get them out of this country" (*Life,* 1994). When she married oil tycoon Aristotle Onassis and moved to Greece, millions of Americans demanded, "How could she do that?" Easily, when you consider that losses "can occasion profound shifts in our sense of who we are, as whole facets of our past that were shared with the deceased slip away from us forever, if only because no one else will ever occupy the unique position in relationship to us necessary to call them forth" (Neimeyer, 1998, p. 90).

Grievers may make choices with radical consequences. For example, by marrying a divorced person, Mrs. Kennedy became estranged from the Roman Catholic Church.

Americans bring their rugged commitment to individualism to grief work. "No two people—not even husband and wife—can be presumed to experience the same grief in response to the same loss" (Neimeyer, 1998, p. 91). A husband may not be disclosing everything that he is thinking and feeling in order to be, or appear to be, strong for his mate or other family members.

Lesson 2: "Grieving is something we do, not something that is done for us" (p. 91).

Generally, Neimeyer argues, grief is an "unwelcomed intruder in our lives" (p. 91). After all, who volunteers for grief? (Suicide survivors can be outraged: How dare you do this to me?) While there are many things a pastor, family members, and church friends can do to support the grieving person, ultimately he or she stands as alone against grief as any gladiator facing an opponent in ancient Rome.

Admittedly, death can make you feel out of control, defenseless, helpless, and abandoned, especially when the person with whom we would have shared this grief is the deceased. This is especially true after long marriages. Neimeyer will have none of this passivity. Grief responses are a choice taken or ignored.

Grievers must deal not only with the primary loss (say, a spouse) but also with the secondary or consequential losses such as dreams, a second paycheck, a sex partner, a helpmate, and a shared future (Harris, 2000). Such multiple losses mean that grievers face a bewildering maze of competing must-be-made-now decisions.

Some Choices Facing a Griever		
View the body	or	Not view the body
Have a funeral	or	Not have a funeral
Share my feelings	or	Keep my feelings bottled up
Go it alone	or	Ask for help
Sell the house	or	Keep the house
Stay here	or	Move to another city

The chief mourner in this period of intense sequential decision-making (and second-guessing) may feel rushed or pressured by potential decisions or by particular advisers. Moreover, some choices have legal and financial repercussions.

Certainly the financial resources of the griever influence decision-making. Consider the decision-making demands on the widow with two children in college who cannot afford to pay the mortgage and upkeep, contrasted to those of the widow whose mortgage insurance and life insurance paid off well.

When will the pain end?

A wrongful death or homicide raises particular questions. Consider the decisions facing parents whose children died in the Columbine High School shootings. Shall I sue or not sue? Who do I sue? Indeed, this can become the major decision affecting those whose loved one died as a result of negligence or medical malpractice.

Attorneys may promise, "We will make *someone* pay for this." What attorneys do not disclose is that the grief will be dragged out through the courts and in the media for years.

The "someone" who pays may be the survivors. Think about the impact of the delay on family members in the Pan Am trial held 12 years after the bombing over Lockerbie, Scotland.

Lesson 3: "Grieving is the act of affirming or reconstructing a personal world of meaning that has been challenged by loss" (p. 92).

Grievers often moan, "I don't know where to begin!" Lives are on hold pending the settling of an estate (particularly if the deceased did not have a will). Surprises ambush the grieving, such as discovering that a spouse had allowed life insurance to lapse, had not changed the beneficiary on a policy from a previous marriage, or was having (or had had) an affair. The death and subsequent changes death sets in motion have the potential to repeatedly sabotage grievers who are trying to make sense of the loss.

Pastor-leaders continually remind the bereaving to include God in the meaning-making process.

Initially grievers ask, "Why?" But the pastor-leader raises another question: "What is God saying to you in your grieving or in this latest development?"

I add, "How can you partner with God to work to bring the best out of what appears to be a mess?" Joan's husband died while they were vacationing in Texas. Although he had great medical insurance, he died "outside the coverage area" according to a letter Joan received from the health management organization denying coverage of more than one half of the medical expenses. Joan finds herself alone and facing more than $70,000 in unpaid hospital and transportation costs. (Moreover, her husband had always handled the money in the family.) Some friends are urging, "Sue 'em!" Is Joan up to a prolonged, expensive legal battle? How good is her case? As her pastor, what would you advise?

> The only useful question in such a time is not "Why?" but "What's next? What should I do next? What should be my response to this ugly event? How can I bring the best out of it?"
> —Frederica Mathewes-Green, 1999, p. 57

When the death is a homicide

Making sense of the death is more difficult when it was the result of a homicide. Assuming an arrest, indictment, and trial, the grievers must deal with a criminal justice system. Some murders go unsolved and leave family and friends in an emotional limbo. Some families end up feeling they are victimized by the legal process.

How does anyone reconstruct a world of meaning when a killer gets off lightly or on a technicality? How does anyone live with the thought, "Something is being covered up"? Given the violence in American culture, increasingly people must live with the reality that those thought or found responsible for the death may never pay full justice. Even with a conviction, how much time will actually be served? The arena for the dispute shifts in some families from the court to the parole process or to civil action. Others come to realize that justice will not bring back a loved one.

Grief as a work in progress

Grievers face two choices in reconstructing meaning:

- graft the loss onto an existing value system, or
- incorporate the loss in a new, revamped value system, or as one husband complained at his wife's reaction, "Just be mad at everyone and everything!"

Lesson 4: "We spontaneously seek opportunities to tell and retell the stories of our loss, and in so doing, recruit social validation for the changed story lines of our lives" (p. 94).

> Daughter: "Why would you want to hear other people's stories?"
> Mother: "So I can have permission to tell my own."
> —Susan Ford Wiltshire, 1994, p. 81

Grievers do important reconstruction work by telling their stories again and again, continuously revising as they go. The key element is what Neimeyer calls "account-making." Grievers weave facts, wonderings, and sometimes fiction into an account of the death. For some, the account may resemble a jigsaw puzzle with missing pieces. Susan Ford Wiltshire suggests that the stories of our loved ones keep getting written and rewritten, not unlike revised editions of reference works. Grievers who find mutual help groups or aftercare groups are fortunate to have a safe place to tell their stories. Some grievers find great help in attending such groups; other family members ask, "What good does that do?"

Grief is like a 1001-piece jigsaw puzzle—only there is no picture to guide you. You have no idea whether this piece of blue is sky, water, or a car. All you know is someone is impatiently demanding, "Come on. Haven't you figured it out yet?"

One reason visitations and aftercare groups are so important is that they provide a safe environment to exchange narratives that lead to a conclusion: "I am *not* the only one!" or "I am *not* going crazy!" Social validation from another griever in response to your own account is one of life's greatest blessings.

All grievers need a safe place to grieve, a space where someone listens with their eyes as well as their hearts. Such a place in Hebrew is called *Mehom hanekhama*—a place of comfort.

What might be termed the "latest draft" will still be further refined. The accounts may well be punctuated by great emotions that the griever can express in the safety of a trusted listener or mutual help group.

In the remodeling of a home and working with a contractor or architect, the plans go through changes and modifications. So it is with a person's grief account. Neimeyer finds that in stage theories, feelings and emotions are seen as "problems to be overcome with the passage of time or the administration of 'treatment'" (p. 94), including drugs. Some grievers, in fact, are hamstrung by the introduction of "comparative grief time." One man suggested, "Yeah, when my dad died I had a hard time for about three months." The implication is "So should you."

As a pastor, how do you see a parishioner's denial? As—

- An inability to assimilate a death at a given point of time? or
- "An attempt to 'suspend' the death until its meaning can be better grasped"? (Neimeyer, 1998, p. 95).

Noted grief scholar Margaret Stroebe contends that it is more reasonable for some individuals to cope by initially suppressing the loss (and reminders of the loss) rather than immediately immersing themselves in "grief work." In fact, she argues, for some, "it may do little good to encourage grief work" (1992-93, p. 35). When they're ready, they'll do their grief work. Some will welcome pastoral assistance or guidance in sorting through their grief experiences. Rather than discover a meaning for a death, by honoring feelings many live their way into a meaning. A pastor-leader is a frequent coach along the way, particularly in the portion that resembles a maze.

Negotiating support

Lesson 5: "We construct and reconstruct our identities as survivors of loss in negotiation with others" (p. 96).

Clearly, just as quarterbacks need receivers to catch the football, grievers need question-receivers for their musings. Grievers once were able to take the promises of support made in a funeral home as social IOUs. Now many grievers recognize them for what they are: socially acceptable clichés. Uncollectable.

Grievers must be like active rafters on the wild river of grief. They are not merely along for the scenery. Someone somewhere knows what you now need to know not just for your own survival but also for the survival of your family and friends. Not surprisingly, many are finding "answers" in grief chat rooms on the Internet.

Recruiting support

Increasingly in the "grief-lite" culture, the griever must recruit a support team to be there for the long haul in a culture that has become impatient with grief and grievers. Support falls into three time categories:

IMMEDIATE/CRISIS ➔ TRANSITIONAL ➔ LONG-TERM

Admittedly, some churches are good at providing immediate crisis care. Members can whip up casseroles or buy buckets of chicken instantly. Someone knows how to organize meals for a week (or a day in some communities). But as grief settles in for the long haul, support drops off. Lois Wyse (1995) divides support into two groups: the *go-ers* and the *stay-ers*. One widow captured it this way: "I couldn't begin to eat all the casseroles that I found in my refrigerator. But after the first few months, I noticed a dramatic decline in 'Just called to see how you are doing' calls and social invitations. By the time I began figuring out what it meant to be a widow, I was getting an astonished, 'What! Are you *still* grieving?'"

Increasingly in American church life, grief is like a debit card: eventually it is used up. The griever will not receive a replacement.

In some losses, such as prenatal death or the death of a senior adult, support may be difficult to recruit because of disenfranchisement. "But you didn't bring the baby to full term!" one pastor informed a young grieving mother. "Your mother lived such a good long life," another pastor told a grieving adult. Both grievers reported feeling they had been scolded. It is not unusual for someone implicitly to disenfranchise a loss.

Pastor-leaders find ways to say to grievers: Your grief counts!

One griever described an encounter soon after the death of his elderly mother whom he had moved into his home so he could provide adequate care for her. He expected his Sunday School teacher to be supportive. At the visitation, the teacher stunned him by saying, "You know, you really are better off with her dead. She was such a drain on you for all these years that she was sick. You haven't been able to use your ministry gifts around the church." John stopped attending Sunday School. "I could never go back to sit under his teaching."

When friends grieve

The "Who am I now?" question is, in many cases, followed up by "Who are *we* now?" Some individuals discover that the friendship with another individual was really the spouse's friend. One widower recalled, "All the time I thought we were friends. I was merely along for the ride." More than one griever has reported of some family members, as well as friends, "Never heard from them again."

When friends say, "You are handling this so well" they may later distance themselves through that assessment: "You don't need our help anymore."

Compliments such as "You're handling this beautifully" may block the griever from appearing to need help.

Friends may ask among themselves, "How is she doing?" and swap insights and puzzlements. One friend's take on the grief may become the perceived reality by others in a congregation. Elizabeth Harper Neeld argues that every griever needs that special someone—"someone who gives us total permission to grieve, who encourages us to talk as much as we wish, to cry, to show our anger. Someone who does not try to make us feel better or urge us to make the

> **As time goes on, it will become even more important that we let our friends and family know what we need . . . We should, therefore, ask for what we need.**
> **—Elizabeth Harper Neeld, 1990, p. 48**

best of what has occurred or attempt to show us the good that is still present in our lives" (1990, p. 49).

Some grievers don't ask for help. When Jimmy Stewart's wife died, the great film actor "withdrew from the world," in his daughter's words. "He didn't know what to do with himself" or with his grief ("No man is poor who has friends," 1997, p. A-2). Four years later, in 1997, Stewart himself died. How much life did he miss during those four years? It has not been uncommon to hear, "He grieved himself to death," although that does not appear on a death certificate.

Effective pastor-leaders model long-term care to congregations.

Some people are different after a loss. It may be difficult for a pastor or members of a congregation to deal with these changes.

Joan Rivers told the New England Conference on Grief in 1997 that after her husband's suicide, some friends pointedly informed her, "We liked the *old* Joan better." Rivers replied, "The old Joan doesn't exist any more!"

Grievers may, in time, come to acquire new friends, supporters, and what I like to call "allies." That may mean auditing a friendship roster and concluding, "These individuals cannot offer what I now need." Admittedly, some will conclude that it's time to move on from a congregation as well, particularly if the individual believes the congregation has failed to be support-

> **Fully engaging in mourning means that you will be a different person from the one you were before you began.**
> **—Anne Brener, 1993, p. 146**

ive. There must be a willingness to find a common ground on which support can be given and received. Some grievers must turn to or seek support from the second tier of assistance. Some have been surprised by who steps forward.

Reconstructing "completion"

For many, the recurring question is "When will my grief be over?"

"Your feelings of loss will not completely disappear, yet they will soften, and the intense pains of grief will become less frequent. Hope for a continued life will emerge as you are able to make commitments to the future. . . . The unfolding of this journey is not intended to create a return to an 'old normal' but the discovery of a 'new normal'" (Wolfelt, 1997, p. 136).

J. William Worden, a leading clinician, answers "How long?" questions by noting that grief changes

- when grievers regain an interest in life
- when grievers feel more hopeful
- when grievers experience gratification again and
- when grievers adapt to new roles (1991, p. 19)

Grievers make up what Lily Pincus calls "the general conspiracy that death has not occurred" (cited in Neeld, 1990, p. 46) as captured in the phrase "Life goes on." In words many professionals do not want to hear, because of the implications for continued care, Worden wisely points out: "There is also a sense in which mourning is never finished" (1991, p. 19).

> **Life doesn't get *better* for grieving parents— it gets *different*.**
> —Dennis Apple, whose son died at age 19

For some, grief is not a lifelong handicap but a learning laboratory. The difference in perception may be gained with the support and guidance of a caring pastor-leader who continues to be present for grievers long after the rituals are concluded, long after the flowers have died, long after friends have moved on. I like the way one country preacher explained grief: "Grief is like the Israelites facing the River Jordan. Sometimes there's no way over it, no way under it, no way around it. The only way is *through* it. Some of the time it's on dry ground. But a lot of the time it's slopping through the mud."

A Spiritual Formation Exercise

Grief expression can make pastoral servants uncomfortable. Read 2 Kings 4:18-37, which describes a grieving mother's encounter with the prophet Elisha.

1. Name several recent grievers that you know personally. Take a moment to reflect on your observations of their grief. If you had to capture your observation of their grief in a word or phrase, what would it be?

Name of griever   Word or phrase that captures his or her grief

_____   _____
_____   _____
_____   _____

2. Try to retell this passage in your own words.
3. Read aloud 2 Kings 4:27: "Leave her alone! She is in bitter distress, but the LORD has hidden it from me and has not told me why."
4. Recall an incident in which you have used the phrase "Leave her alone" to someone encountering a griever.
5. Has there been an experience in your ministry in which a griever's distress was hidden from you? Go back to the list above. Take a moment and pray for each person. Ask God to open your heart to any distress that griever might be experiencing.
6. When was the last time you specifically spoke with a griever about his or her grief journey? Do you need to make a pastoral visit to any of these grievers?

A Story That Will Preach

Eleanor Roosevelt, as the First Lady of the United States from 1933 to 1945, had a close relationship with the press and could always be expected to provide a quote. After her husband's death, reporters naturally asked, "Mrs. Roosevelt, what's next?" With an uncharacteristic aloofness, she dismissed their question with "The story is over" and walked away.

What the public did not know in those immediate days after the death of her husband—and would not know until after her death 20 years later—was that the president had not been alone when he died at the Little White House in Warm Springs, Georgia. An old romantic flame had been with him. Mrs. Roosevelt had thought her husband's relationship with the woman had ended 25 years earlier. Yet for the funeral, under public scrutiny, Mrs. Roosevelt had to play the part of the grieving widow (Lash, 1972) mourning for the wartime hero. Her mourning was shaped by seething anger not just at her husband but at Secret Service agents who had "looked the other way" and at her daughter Anna, who had arranged the rendezvous with "the other woman."

Contrary to what she told the reporters, the story was *not* over. Over her objections, succeeding president Harry Truman appointed her to the United States delegation at the founding of the United Nations. For two decades, Mrs. Roosevelt worked tirelessly in global humanitarian causes.

It may appear that "the story is over," but a new story could be beginning.

A Leadership Decision

As a result of reflecting after reading this chapter, I want to

1. _____

2. _____

7
Rediscovering God After Loss

Eternity will have *to last a long time—*
I have enough questions to fill up a thousand years.
—Doug Manning, 1979, p. 47

Key Point Summary
Humans spend their lives constructing and reconstructing a uniquely personalized world of meaning. Death, however, can make shambles of "this world." The more tragic the death, the more troublesome the collision with beliefs. Commonly, two questions are raised:
- **Who is God?**
- **Who is God *now* that grief has touched my life?**

A griever must learn what it means to "be me" without a loved one. Christian grievers must now learn what it means to live the Christian life with a wounding loss.

Reconstructing beliefs about God after loss

"Loss may call the existence of God into question. Pain seems to conceal him from us, making it hard for us to believe that there could be a God in the midst of our suffering. In our pain we are tempted to reject God, yet for some reason we hesitate to take that course of action. So we ponder and pray. We move toward God, then away from him" (Sittser, 1995, p. 144).

God and death

Many grievers mumble after a death, "How could God let something like this happen?" Others confess, "Nothing I have believed about God makes sense now." Observing Christians may conclude, "This is all part of God's plan. Someway He will use this for His glory." When the latter interpretation is publicly stated or is relayed to the griever, it may incite an angry reaction, "How can the death of _____ glorify God?" The enemy will use that question like an endless phone prompt that annoys the waiting caller.

> **God Questions Arise**
> - when a family member or friend believes (and says) "God *took* my loved one"
> - when a family member or friend believes (and says) "God *allowed* my loved one to die" or "God could have prevented this!"
> - when a family member or friend asks, "Why *didn't* God prevent this?"

No one experiences death in a vacuum, but rather in a particular cultural context. The theology we rely on in crisis "reflects the biases and filters of our own time and place" (Lyman, 1999, p. 107). "Christians in every generation struggle to express their faith" and grief "through their interpretation of scripture and the values of their own society and experience" (p. 107).

Singing beliefs

Many Christians verbalize their theology by singing. At the close of his son's funeral, my friend Dennis Apple stood and said, "In my family, when we go through a tough experience, we sing." So on that cold February afternoon we sang. Cole observes, "Hymns enable us to make connections with important learnings and to reinforce our understandings. Hymns are frequently the mode by which we store ideas and feelings deep in our memories" (2000, p. 24; citing Adey, 1986, p. 1).

For more than two centuries Christians have sung "How Firm a Foundation." The traditional third stanza reads,

> *When thro' the deep waters I call thee to go,*
> *The rivers of sorrow shall not overflow;*
> *For I will be with thee thy trials to bless,*
> *And sanctify to thee thy deepest distress.*
> —John Rippon

Interaction

Grievers interact in their grief drama in the following roles.

Defenders: They feel they must zealously protect God, particularly on the turf of a funeral home or cemetery and in the bereaved's home. Death and grief are times to draw a line in the sand to prevent "theological error."

Antagonists: They believe grief to be an ideal season to launch a blitzkrieg of cynical questions, many of which are unanswerable and do little to comfort the grieving. In fact, their statements are seeds that over time become ripe and confuse the bereaving and derail grief work.

The pastor-leader must walk or navigate among these grievers and their questions, sometimes deciding, "This is not the time or the place for theological argument." Dialogue, yes; arguments, no.

As one pastor graciously told a griever, "Robert, I am going to pray to the God you say you no longer believe in, to reach out to you in your grief." The pastor-leader acknowledges the questions but rarely debates the existence or ways of God.

God after Columbine

Fourteen students and one teacher died in the shootings at Columbine High School in Littleton, Colorado, in 1999. Because of the extensive media coverage, a local incident became a national tragedy and prompted a lively discussion not only on gun control and safety in schools but also on the sovereignty of God. Some assigned meaning by seeing "martyrdom" in those students believed to have died for professing their faith.

Time reexamined the tragedy in an article titled "A Surge of Teen Spirit" with this secondary headline: "A Christian girl, martyred at Columbine High, sparks a revival among many evangelical teens" (*Time,* May 31, 1999, p. 58). Little wonder that one slain student's biography was titled *She Said "Yes": The Unlikely Martyrdom of Cassie Bernall.* Kenneth Woodward suggests that those who advance the martyrdom interpretation assume "Cassie's death was part of God's plan to bring forth witnesses out of the Columbine killings who would then win others to Christ" (June 14, 1999, p. 64). One Columbine student, Erika Dendorfer, concludes, "At the memorial service for Cassie, 60 kids gave their lives to Christ" (Haines, July 29, 1999, p. 9). To some, these conversions prove the truth of Rom. 8:28. Realistically, that which comforts one griever may annoy another. Some parents whose children died, or individuals whose friends died, might not be as ready to so interpret the death.

> **The underlying—even if unspoken—question is, if God acts like this, could this happen to me or someone I love?**

In this age when many want a predictable God, such widely mediacized deaths become opportunities for pastoral response. A pastor-leader responds courageously and sensitively.

Troublesome deaths

Gamino, Sewell, and Easterling, in a study of 85 grievers, identified three significant situational variables that influence grief experience: (1) traumatic death, (2) younger age of the deceased, and (3) the perception of preventability. Pastoral leadership becomes complicated when grievers have a history of mental instability, substance abuse, and a great number of other losses.

Out-of-order deaths (the suicide of a mate, the tragic drowning of a child at camp, an automobile accident killing a bride and groom, or random violence that takes the lives of adolescents) can powerfully "challenge the adequacy of our most cherished beliefs and taken-for-granted ways of life" (Neimeyer, 1998, p. 88). Such deaths position many grievers for a collision with their beliefs about the goodness of God. Newlyweds are supposed to head off for a blissful honeymoon, not die in a car wreck. Children are supposed to grow up and one day bury their parents. So where was God when such deaths happened? That question is followed by "Where is God in our bereavement?"

Early in the loss, the griever may be trusting that Jesus cares. Only through the inevitable hammering on the anvil of bereavement does that trust turn into conviction.

One way He demonstrates that care is through pastors who lead in grief, pastors who prayerfully make themselves available to grievers.

These days, particularly in large churches, some believe that the pastor is too busy to deal with them. Many initiate conversations with "Pastor, I hate to interrupt you. I know you're so busy." God demonstrates care through pastor-leaders who respond, "I have all the time you need."

Sometimes a griever wonders, "Am I the *only* person in this family [or this church or youth group] who is angry at God?" When grievers cannot verbalize questions or own their feelings, particularly when they are shamed for their honesty—"if you really were a Christian" or "where you should be spiritually"—the questioners suffer in isolation.

When accusations sting

Some turn their anger onto others, particularly if someone tries to dismiss their questions with "It is not for us to ask why." Just as Dubin and Sarnoff report that bereaving persons unleash hostile and angry feelings toward health professionals, they also direct those feelings toward pastors and counselors. It takes a wise pastor-leader not to take the remarks personally. Outbursts may signal guilt or unresolved conflict with the deceased (Vanezis and McGee, 1999) rather than with anything the pastor has done or failed to do. So pastor-leaders respond, "I hear you. I want to understand what you're feeling and thinking."

Many pastors have left emergency rooms, funeral homes, cemeteries, or private residences bruised by the reception to offered pastoral care. While it's tempting to replay hostility or accusations, the pastor-leader commits the accusation and accuser into God's loving care and invites the Holy Spirit to guard the heart and mind from taking offense.

The pastor-leader seeks to create a bridge back into this griever's life, what one might call "the ministry of a second opportunity."

A family member's pastor may be hundreds of miles away at the time of the loved one's death or funeral. Thus, another pastor offers emergency or initial spiritual care. Chloe Breyer suggests that pastors sometimes function "more like emergency room staff—ready to sew up spiritual wounds" sufficiently to get the griever through the funeral and committal before passing the griever "along to the primary [spiritual] care providers" (2000, p. 862). Unfortunately, there may be little contact between the pastors involved or follow up in offering grief care when this happens.

Giving permission to be angry at God

Reg Johnson, dean of the chapel at Asbury Theological Seminary, offers grievers permission through a simple but profound statement: "God never chides his children for being children."

The wise pastor-leader is alert to camouflaged or submerged spiritual questions. The right question is often an invitation for the griever to "own up" to discomforting spiritual beliefs.

An absence of immunity

Pastors and theologians have no immunity to grief or doubts. Paraphrasing Thomas Paine, there are losses that try pastors' souls. One pastor describes his reaction at a critical point in a building program, when the dynamic chairman died:

"Why?" I pleaded. "Why *now*? I need him—this church needs him."

But I had preached his funeral without admitting to a soul my questions, my anger. I wanted to be open with my congregation, to reveal my doubts. I listened to several express the questions that I could not verbalize. I wanted, for once, to say, "This morning, this preacher doesn't have answers—only questions." But I didn't. I ignored my pain and did a funeral that got a lot of "Thank you, Pastor" comments. But I felt beaten up by the experience. By God's help we made it through the funeral and eventually into the new building. But to this day I still wonder why.

C. S. Lewis gained the reputation during World War II as something of an authority on suffering. After the deaths of his close friend, poet

Charles Williams, and Lewis's wife, Joy, the Oxford professor confessed, "I thought I trusted the rope until it mattered to me whether it would bear me. Now it matters, and I find I didn't" (Lewis, 1961, p. 43). Once consigned to the laboratory of grief (some insist the prison of grief), Lewis reexamined his most cherished assumptions as well as the answers he had given on the lecture circuit and in his books. Like many Christians, he defined the deaths as instruments "sent to try us" (p. 61). To some, he reasoned, grief becomes the grand experiment of their faith: "God has not been trying an experiment on my faith or love in order to find out their quality. He knew it already. It was I who didn't. In this trial He makes us occupy the dock, the witness box, and the bench all at once. He always knew that my temple was a house of cards. His only way of making me realize the fact was to knock it down" (p. 61).

Questions

Grievers can grill clergy in the rapid-fire manner of a seasoned prosecutor—"How could an all-powerful God let this happen?"—particularly in an era with great enthusiasm for angels. "So, Pastor, where were the guardian angels?" In fact, some people link questions to a particular scripture: "He will command his angels concerning you to guard you in all your ways" (Ps. 91:11). After a friend died and I was reminded of this scripture, I asked a noted authority on angels, "Is it possible to have a klutz for a guardian angel?" Lewis reminds us, "My idea of God is not a divine idea. It has to be shattered time after time" (Lewis, 1961, p. 76). Our neatly packaged beliefs must be shattered so that we may find the real God very present with us in this loss.

> **One of the distinctions of Christianity is**
> **a God who suffers alongside us.**

The promise of future understanding

Many grievers consider clergy to be "field reps" for God. Most ministers feel uncomfortable or defensive undergoing such a grilling, particularly in public (you never know when someone is eavesdropping) and spontaneous. It takes grace to respond compassionately to an anguished "God could have saved my loved one's life but didn't! *Why?*" Generations of pastor-leaders have pointed to the truth in the gospel hymn that states "We will understand it better by and by."

This hope of future understanding is indeed found in numerous gospel songs and funeral homilies. Nevertheless, such lyrics anger some grievers. Many adults have never closely reflected on their beliefs about death, heaven, eternity, or resurrection until confronted by the death of a loved one. In the crucible of grief, these questions may be all they can think about or want to discuss.

The problem is not the questions. It's to whom the questioner turns for answers. It's possible that the answer-giver has never been directly touched by death.

Second, some answer-givers offer easy answers. While writing this book, I attended a funeral of a six-year-old who died of leukemia. The pastor did not touch the "Why?" that filled the funeral home. He offered grievers a dazzling theological treatise on the sovereignty of God. He left satisfied, but the rest of us did not. While we may take comfort in the words of the Nicene Creed, "We look for the resurrection of the dead, and the life of the world to come," grievers must live with a question strewn from now until they get to "sweet by and by" and "the resurrection of the dead."

Few pastors can escape the temptation to dodge rather than engage a griever's questions; some grievers are energized and others paralyzed by a spiritual quest for answers. Pastors have sometimes left such encounters convinced that the griever understood their answers; in reality, the griever was simply too polite to ask again.

Thomas Oden said, "The experienced minister knows that the times of approaching death and bereavement are exceptional opportunities for spiritual growth" (1983, p. 297). And for spiritual chaos. Spiritual growth may come after vigorous grappling with the questions; rarely will it come by ducking the questions. Gerald Sittser, whose mother, wife, and daughter died in the same automobile accident, reflects: "Sorrow took up permanent residence in my soul . . . and enlarged it" (1995, p. 37). One way the soul is enlarged is through honest engagement with the questions in the absence of answers.

The pastor-leader recognizes that bereavement can be opportunities for spiritual defeat, even despair. Grievers may well have a Ps. 137 moment: "For there our captors asked us for songs, our tormenters demanded songs of joy" (v. 3). Many grievers have essentially paraphrased the psalmist in verse 4, "How shall we sing the Lord's song in a strange land *called grief?*"

Historically, Christians sang their grief. Hymnals in the last century commonly had dozens of songs about death and grief. Now it's hard to identify even one praise chorus with the theme of death.

Your attitude may be showing

Answers can be theologically and scripturally precise, but the attitude of the answer-giver is sometimes perceived as uncaring. Little surprise that a hymn by Jeremiah E. Rankin, after posing the question "Do you fear the gath'ring clouds of sorrow?" advises "Tell it to Jesus *alone*" (emphasis added). A number of songs support this guidance: "Have a Little Talk with Jesus," "On the Jericho Road," and "I Must Tell Jesus." The latter reflects, at least in the chorus, the going-it-alone individualism: "Jesus can help me, Jesus *alone*" (emphasis added).

How do you receive questions from grievers? The pastor-manager sees such questions as an imposition, a task. The pastor-*leader* hears the question as an invitation and an opportunity for compassion.

The pastor-leader knows that any question may be attached to a string of questions, not unlike scarfs a magician pulls from his or her sleeve. Yet the pastor does not begrudge time spent being pastorally faithful. Pastor-leaders honor the griever behind the questions.

To be clear, "answers" take little of a pastor's time. Being willing to hear the question all the way to the question mark can eat up a lot of time in a busy pastor-leader's day. Making time for a griever's questions is a key ingredient in offering hospitality to the grieving. Time spent with these questions may lead to the real question emotionally and spiritually menacing the griever.

Reconstructing beliefs about heaven and hell

The Gallup Organization in its 1997 study of American spiritual beliefs about dying also looked into beliefs about the afterlife. Their discovery is insightful to pastors: "Most Americans believe that they will exist in some form after death; the experience is positive; that they will be on a journey of some kind; will experience spiritual growth; and that the quality of existence will depend on things done in one's life and one's spiritual state at the time of death" (Gallup study on spiritual beliefs, 1997, p. 14).

Even heaven (which 7 people out of 10 tell the Gallup Organization they believe in) means different things to different people.

I really don't think of heaven so much as a place of rest and golden streets as I think of heaven as a place where I can serve God unshackled by my present limitations of finiteness which so often get in my way.
—**Christie, cited in Sue Howard and Gail Howard, 1973, p. 25**

J. William Worden, recognized as a leading grief theorist, believes that one of the critical tasks of grievers is to "emotionally relocate the deceased" (1991, p. 16). I recall the anguish expressed in one of my Grief

Gatherings by a father who was deeply troubled because he wasn't sure of his son's salvation. "I think my son went to hell," he said.

Eternity takes on a different dimension when you are trying to "spiritually locate" a loved one. Especially when someone asks the key question, "Where is he [she] *now?*" Committing a loved one into God's hands is seldom a one-time, but rather a recurring, experience.

Heaven takes on a new meaning when loved ones die; in reality, until that point, heaven for many was rather abstract or sentimental. I have a clearer, stronger belief in heaven after the death of my parents than ever before. While I don't understand all the details of the promise, I do trust the *One* who promises, "I am going there to prepare a place for you" (John 14:2).

But how do you explain heaven to a child? How do you as a spiritual leader "clean up" a botched explanation without undermining the authority of a parent or grandparent who offered it? Maria Shriver wrestled with her children's questions after the death of their great-grandmother Rose Kennedy. Maria's struggling led her to write the book *What's Heaven?* in which a mother answers a child's questions. In one place she wrote, "I believe that if you're good throughout your life, then you get to go to heaven. Some people believe in different kinds of heaven and have different names for it" (1999, no pagination).

Take a moment and reread Shriver's words. Any red flags pop up in your mind? Then what resources do you have on your shelf to explain heaven to a child? What resources do your Sunday School teachers or daycare teachers have? Remember: people give books to children without having read them carefully or completely. Some adults struggle with answering the questions of children, particularly when a child's question reignites their own questions.

The issue becomes more complex when individuals (of all ages) ask about the awareness of the dead. Shriver writes, "She is watching over us from up there." For some this sounds like Santa Claus—"He knows when you've been bad or good." For others it is menacing. Wisdom from C. S. Lewis may prove helpful: "Heaven will solve our problems, I think, but not by showing us subtle reconciliations between all our apparently contradictory notions. The notions will all be knocked from under our feet. We shall see that there never was any problem" (1961, p. 83).

Condensing the issue

Many pastors would vigorously refute Shriver's words: "It's not about being 'good' throughout our lives." For many the issue is simply "Was the deceased saved or born-again? Had the deceased accepted Jesus as his or her personal Lord and Savior?" In some cases there is confident clarity, that is, the testimony of the deceased; in other cases there is troubling uncertainty. Some feel responsibility for not having witnessed to the deceased or for never having inquired about the deceased's relationship with God. For others, the details of conversion are unclear.

A tension exists between mainline and Evangelical Christians, as well as between Christians and those who practice other world religions. Among some, being a good person, being a church member, or having been baptized or confirmed is good enough

> Melvin McCullough, pastor of First Church of the Nazarene in Bethany, Oklahoma, suggests that Christians can do their pastors a big favor in preparing to preach funerals: "Write out your conversion experience and include that with your funeral documents. That way, the pastor is supplied with a clear testimony of salvation. These written words can refresh your pastor's memory of personal conversations with the deceased. You can help your pastor 'preach' your own funeral."
>
> —Melvin McCullough, 1999

for general admission. If you believe in the eternal security of the believer, as expressed in the phrase "once saved, always saved," all you need is a "Come into my heart, Lord Jesus" moment. Indeed, the thrust of some pastoral interactions with the dying is "Get 'em to pray the sinner's prayer." But deathbed conversions can be second-guessed long after the funeral.

More than once after a funeral I heard my dad complain, "He [the minister] preached him right into heaven." Robert Blair, writing after a long career as a minister in a conservative denomination, offers this perspective: "I have established some principles for myself. First, I don't attempt to relegate anyone to hell or install anyone in the heavenly realms . . . to assign a heavenly berth or cubicle of hell is not our place. I can't say for sure that anyone will be in heaven; only the Lord truly knows who are his. However, I can relate the person's witness of his or her faith" (1998, p. 28).

Years ago, I learned this paradox: "There will be three surprises in heaven: (1) that I am there; (2) those who are there whom I didn't expect to be there; and (3) who are not there whom I expected to be there. Blair summarizes the position of many clergy: "We can never be sure where a person's heart is" (p. 67).

Whatever happened to hell?

My dad often testified of his belief that "there is a heaven to gain and a hell to shun." Many clergy of a certain age were exposed to fervent descriptions of hell; these days, perhaps as something of a reaction to that exposure, some pastors cannot recall the last sermon they preached on hell. Thus, many Christians cannot remember the last sermon they heard on hell. The theology of hell is becoming increasingly fuzzy.

Hell has become something of an embarrassment to many Christians. British grief scholar Tony Walter, one of the few thanatologists to raise the touchy subject, suggests that the "hell" of two world wars defanged hell. He points to a subtle shift among Evangelicals, a "keeping quiet about hell." In fact, he links the demise of hell to family values: "Hope of reunion with kin has undermined the power of the churches." Simply, "At the popular level it was hell's incompatibility with automatic family reunion that led to its demise" (1999, p. 47). The subtle implication is that nonbelievers do not go to hell but simply cease to exist.

Pastoral counselors see individuals who had complicated relationships with particular family members and who now express great anxiety about a future reconciliation in heaven. One woman whose father died without ever seeking her forgiveness for years of molestation said, "I didn't shed a tear when he died. But I can't imagine spending eternity with him after what he did to me." Such confessions and the anxiety behind them must be treated with a great deal of care. If death can invalidate our beliefs, we may well need someone who can hear out our questions and witness our struggle to live with the unanswered, even taunting "Why?" questions. Grievers need someone who can be patient rather than outraged with "temporary atheism." Sadly, some grievers will never express their doubts, even disbelief. They go on about their business, even attending church. But in quiet moments they wrestle with the loss: "I just wish I knew for sure that he was safe." Although pastors have "committed" the deceased into the hands of a loving God, for some grievers that's not enough.

Goal of Pastoral Leadership

The pastor-leader receives the grief of the bereaving and listens to what is said about God and to what is not said. The pastor-leader is actively present with grievers and their questions.

A Spiritual Formation Exercise

1. Take some time to read John 11:1-32 once more. Ask God to bless your reading.

2. In your mind turn over these words of Mary and Martha, "Lord, . . . if you had been here, my brother would not have died" (v. 21).
3. Say these words to express different emotions: (1) anger, (2) dripping irony, (3) politeness, (4) hurtfulness, and (5) ambivalence.
4. In what ways do Mary and Martha "reconstruct" their view of Jesus now that Lazarus has died?
5. Think about grievers in your congregation. Who has said, in essence, "Lord, if You had *come through,* my loved one would not have died?" What in this passage might be helpful to them?

A Story That Will Preach

The White House was in commotion that Friday night in 1963, hours after President John Kennedy had been assassinated in Dallas. As dignitaries arrived by limousine and helicopter for a hastily convened cabinet meeting, John Kennedy Jr. danced like any impatient three-year-old— "Daddy's home! Daddy's home!" Someone had decided that the Irish nanny, Maude Shaw, should break the news to the children since she had done such a good job telling them of their brother Patrick's death just three months earlier. But repeatedly she postponed the task: "I haven't the heart to tell them . . . why can't someone else do this? I can't. I can't."

Now she would find a way to tell them that their father, the president, was dead. She would find a strength in her strong faith to do the impossible. But as many others that dark November night, Maude, too, was asking, "Why?" Finally, six-year-old Caroline, noticing the tears streaming down Miss Shaw's face, asked, "Why are you so sad?"

Maude began to tell Caroline some of the facts: "Your father has been shot. They took him to a hospital, but they couldn't make him better." Then out of her Irish Catholic spirituality, she sought a way to help this little girl understand.

"He's gone to look after Patrick. Patrick was so lonely in heaven. He didn't know anyone there. Now he has the best friend anyone could have. And your father will be so very glad to see Patrick" (Andersen, 2000, p. 73).

A little voice interrupted, "But what will Daddy *do* in heaven?"

"I'm sure God is giving him enough things to do, because he was always such a very busy man. God has made your daddy a guardian angel for you and for Mommy and for John."

That little girl cried herself to sleep in a bed in the White House, just as many did across the nation that awful November night. Even residents of 1600 Pennsylvania Avenue are not immune from the realities of life. Nor are they immune from questioning how a good God could allow such a thing to happen. Nor are they immune from revisiting *initial* explanations.

But what about John? How do you explain death to a three-year old? And what about his upcoming birthday party? The next morning, Maude Shaw broke the news to him. John asked two questions, "Did Daddy take his big plane with him?"

"Yes."

"I wonder when he's coming back."

Nannies can do a lot, but how do you answer a question like that? Just as nannies, pastors are asked unanswerable questions. Sometimes statements are questions. Martha's observation, "Lord, if you had been here, my brother would not have died," is a disguised accusation that must have stung Jesus: Why weren't You here? Why didn't You come when we sent for You? What could have been more important than us? Jesus could have sidestepped the confrontation by making a beeline to the grave site and then walking Lazarus home. But Jesus gave two friends the chance to ask, *Where have You been?*

Jesus did not scold His friends for their questions. He honored their grief and even joined in with them when He wept—a point pastor-leaders never forget.

How the griever's questions are honored and answered go a long way toward demonstrating pastoral leadership. So how do you as a busy pastor "receive" the questions of the grieving?

A Leadership Decision

As a result of reflecting after reading this chapter, I want to

1. _____

2. _____

When disaster strikes, understanding of God is at risk. Unexpected illness or death, national catastrophe, social disruption, personal loss, plague or epidemic, devastation by flood or drought, turn men and women who haven't given God a thought in years into instant theologians. Rumors fly: "God is absent"…"God is angry"…"God is playing favorites, and I'm not the favorite"…"God is ineffectual…"

It is the task of the prophet to stand up at such moments of catastrophe and clarify who God is and how he acts. If the prophet is good—that is, accurate and true—the disaster becomes a lever for…setting them free for God.

—Eugene H. Peterson, 2000, *The Message: Old Testament Prophets*, p. 462

8

Making Prayer

Grief has a way of plundering our prayer life,
leaving us feeling immobile and empty.
—Joyce Rupp, 1988, p. 79

Key Point Summary
The key resource in a pastor-leader's ministry with the griev-
ing is prayer. The pastor-leader prays openly, boldly, cre-
atively, and confidently.

Rupp's observation that grief plunders our prayer life applies not just to the primary griever but also to the secondary griev-er: the pastor-leader. Many pastors in deep distress have prayed, *Lord, I need help with this one.* The historic advice "Take it to the Lord in prayer" is wise for grievers and pastors alike. From the first moments of notification, the pastor-leader is praying, *Lord, guide me.*

> I believe that instead of running from these good-byes, we need to take the time to reflect upon them, to "pray them." In doing so we can become wiser, deeper and more compassionate.
> —Joyce Rupp, 1988, p. 13

Pray

James writes clearly, "Is any one of you in trouble? Let him pray" (5:13). Many pastor-leaders know well the words of the spiritual, "Not my brother, nor my sister, but it's *me,* O Lord, standing in the need of prayer."

Pastor-leaders have learned the accuracy of the statement that
sometimes the most honest prayer is two words: "O God."

Prayers are identified by D. Unruh as "strategic social action" (1983, p. 349)—something we can do when we don't know what else to do. How many times have would-be comforters asked a griever, "What can I do for you?" How many have answered, "Pray. Please pray"? I love these words of reminder from Thomas Merton: "Prayer is not an old woman's idle amusement. Properly understood and applied, it is the most potent instrument of action" (1965, p. 70). More important than a funeral sermon? More important than counseling skills? Yes—definitely yes. The hymn asks well, "Did you stop to pray?"

> **It is one of the great ironies of our human experience that at the time when we most need to experience the tender compassion and strengthening comfort of our God, we very often feel a great distance in this relationship.**
> —Joyce Rupp, 1988, p. 80

It is not surprising that Paul counseled the Ephesians, "Pray in the Spirit on all occasions with all kinds of prayers and requests. With this in mind, be alert and always keep on praying for all the saints" (Eph. 6:18). Even veteran pastors have difficulty praying at times. From the five ministers who participated in my doctoral research—and numerous clergy friends—I am reminded that clergy are not immune from prayer frustration. After one difficult funeral, a pastor lamented, "I know what I'm supposed to believe, but right now I honestly don't know what I *do* believe." The pastor's anxiety was heightened because he had to deliver the funeral homily and act as if his beliefs were unshaken. Another pastor told me that if one more close friend died, he would leave the pastorate for another career.

Words from an ancient hymn guide pastor-leaders:

> *Commit thou all thy griefs*
> *And ways into his hands.*
> *God hears thy sighs and counts thy tears;*
> *God shall lift up thy head.*
> —Paul Gerhardt

History of prayer and grief

First-century Christians created new funeral traditions by borrowing from other sources, especially Judaism (Meeks, 1983). Christians modified the funeral meal of the Romans into Eucharist at the tomb. Christians altered the custom of putting a coin in the mouth of the deceased (to pay the toll to Charon on the ferry across the river Styx) by placing a piece of the Eucharistic bread in the mouth of the deceased (Upton, 1990). The Jewish prayers for fasting days became the foundation of the oldest Christian prayer for the dead, *Commendatio Animae:* "Deliver, O Lord, the soul of thy servant" (Aries, 1974, p. 98).

Early Christians believed the final disposition of a believer's body was a congregational matter (Caspari, 1949). Many had been rejected by their families for embracing the new faith, so friendship took on new importance as Christians embraced concepts called "the family of believers" (Gal. 6:10), "the household of faith," or "the family of God." Part of the new family responsibility was praying for fellow believers in grief.

The early Christians gathered in the home to pray as they washed and anointed the body with oils before wrapping it in white linen (Davies, 1986). As the body was carried to the grave, hymns and psalms were sung and prayed. Christian friends not only privately prayed for the deceased but also gathered for prayer services on the 3rd, 9th, and 40th days after the death as well as on the one-year anniversary of the death (Caspari, 1949).

Eventually masses included the reading of the names of the faithful departed since the church did not recognize a wide gap between the Church Triumphant and the Church Universal. Names of the dead—originally the heroes, martyrs, and bishops—were inscribed on ivory tablets called *diptychs* (Banker, 1988). These lists were read in mass after the list of the saints (Aries, 1974), because it was assumed that, after purgation, friends and loved ones joined the saints in heaven. The Early Church aggressively prayed for their dead. Augustine more than any Early Church father propagated the practice, which, over time, evolved into scandal.

The protest of Martin Luther and the Reformers

Martin Luther and others were outraged by the excesses of praying for the dead. Luther launched his protest with the confident pronouncement, "The just shall live by faith" (Rom. 1:17, KJV), which appealed to the hearts and minds of many who could not afford to pay continually for masses for the deceased.

If salvation is, as Luther preached, *sola gratia,* solely by grace, how could good works or prayers by friends or confraternities who specifically prayed for the dead and cared for widows and orphans benefit the dead? Luther vigorously denounced vigils, requiems, funeral pomp, and purgatory as "popish abominations" (Niebergall and Lathrop, 1986) totally without influence. Among Luther's followers, for a period of time, burial was left up to family and friends; clergy were present only as spectators. Toward the end of his life, Luther reconsidered his stance: "The dead are still our

> When you have prayed once or twice, then let it be sufficient, and commend them unto God.
> —Martin Luther (cited in Leon Wieseltier, 1998, p. 192)

brothers and have not fallen from our community by death; we still remain members of a single body; therefore, it is one of the duties of 'civic neighbourliness' to accompany the dead to the grave" (p. 125).

In many areas of 17th-century Germany, there were no funerals for a period, only silent internments—once reserved for notorious sinners and suicides. The deceased's body was carried to the grave and buried in absolute silence, without prayers, sermons, or singing; some Reformers buried their dead either late at night or at midnight. Such sterile burials (Dunlop, 1993) complicated grief among friends, particularly for those who remained loyal to Rome. Had not friends died trusting them to pray for their souls? Certainly, some resolved the conflict by praying for the dead privately.

The contention of the Reformers that prayers and money did nothing for the dead not only challenged the teachings of the Church but also depleted its coffers, creating financial upheaval all the way to Rome (McLean, 1996). Tony Walter argues that the Protestants' zeal to ban "intercourse between this world and the next" (1999, p. 47) inevitably led to an unforseen secularism. "Protestantism's reluctance to pray for the soul led to funerals that focused increasingly (in the 18th and 19th centuries) on the corpse, the coffin, and the paraphernalia that went with the coffin" (p. 135). The Reformation also set in motion new attitudes toward housing the dead, creating public cemeteries beyond the control of the church.

Prayer resources

Some grievers question the effectiveness of prayer, particularly those who prayed intently for their loved one to live. Since it may be awhile before a griever feels like praying or feels that it has any results, church friends must pray for the grieving as someone like a spiritual proxy (Rupp, 1988). There are several prayer resources:

The Lord's Prayer. Many grievers pray the Lord's Prayer when they cannot find the words to create their own prayers. The opening "Our Father" reminds us of the social reality of death: Any death has implications beyond the family or close friend networks.

"Breathprayers." In the tough seconds of a funeral, those moments of "What am I doing here?" "What am I going to say?" can be confidence-crushing. Pastor-leaders "breathpray." What do we often say to someone in a crisis? "Take a deep breath." Pastor-leaders inhale on words like *O Lord, You are my God* and exhale on *Help me to glorify You in this situation—not just "get through this," but in my actions may You be honored.* Breathprayers can have a remarkable calming impact on a pastor but also on grievers. In fact, the Lord's Prayer (Matt. 6:9-13, KJV) can be prayed in a breathprayer format:

Breathing in	Our Father
Breathing out	which art in heaven,
Breathing in	Hallowed
Breathing out	be thy name.

Breathing in	Thy kingdom come.
Breathing out	Thy will be done
Breathing in	in earth,
Breathing out	as it is in heaven.
Breathing in	Give us this day
Breathing out	our daily bread.
Breathing in	And forgive us our debts,
Breathing out	as we forgive our debtors.
Breathing in	And lead us not into temptation,
Breathing out	but deliver us from evil:
Breathing in	For thine is the kingdom,
Breathing out	and the power,
Breathing in	and the glory,
Breathing out	for ever. Amen.

Share this resource with grievers

Communal prayer. Grievers in all faiths use individual *and* collective prayer: "It is extremely important to come together as friends, for in grief we need others" (Stuart, 1992, p. 130). Catholics come together to pray the rosary or for a prayer service at the visitation. Reciting the Rosary motivates Catholic friends to gather at a particular hour rather than drifting in over the course of the wake. Through this communal prayer, grievers are reminded that they are part of a faith community of friends who pray intentionally.

Although pastor-leaders want to be sensitive about public prayer, fear of offending someone has turned visitations into secular events. I think Protestants have lost a valuable resource in not having a prayer service or at least moments of public prayer as part of the visitation, particularly at the beginning. If we can pray at a school flagpole, why not in a funeral home? And I mean pray, not just dash out "a word of prayer."

Prayer does not have to be predicated on faith. It can also be predicated on need especially when "we are angry at God and the way in which the universe delivers its blows" (Stuart, 1992, p. 154). Leo Rosten recalls the Jewish proverb, "Praying can do no harm" (1977, p. 366). Sometimes an individual wants to be prayed for if not prayed with.

> **Just as there are no atheists in foxholes,**
> **there are few atheists in funeral parlors.**

At the close of each night of visitation for my mother, I gathered the whole family at the casket and prayed. I have, however, observed pastors praying with some grievers but excluding others.

The kaddish. One of the great spiritual treasures of Judaism is the griever's kaddish:

GLORIFIED and sanctified be God's great name throughout the world, which He has created according to His will. May He establish His kingdom within your lifetime and within the lifetime of the whole house of Israel, speedily and soon, and let us say, Amen.

MAY His great name be praised unto all eternity.

EXALTED and praised, glorified and adored, extolled and revered be the name of the Holy One. Blessed is He beyond all song and psalm, beyond all praise mortal man can bestow upon him, and let us say, Amen.

MAY life and abundant peace descend from heaven upon us and all Israel, and let us say, Amen.

MAY the Creator of heavenly peace bestow peace upon us and all Israel, and let us say, Amen.

—Alfred J. Kolatch, 1993, p. 332

Jews traditionally recite the kaddish three times a day during the seven days of initial grief, *shiva*. The kaddish is a community function because a *minyan* or group of 10 (males in Orthodox Judaism, 10 of either gender in other Jewish sects) is required.

Jews consider it essential that a son or daughter pray the kaddish for his or her own parents. Leon Wieseltier reports that although he had not prayed in 20 years, when his father died he prayed the kaddish for the traditional observed period of 11 months minus one day.

Joining mourners to pray the kaddish provides a rationale for friends to visit the home (to be part of the *minyan*) and to visit at mealtime (to bring food). The kaddish gives socially sanctioned permission to remember (Syme, 1988) and grieve long after Christians have been expected to stop.

One byproduct of praying is that in prayer friends may think of something to do or to offer to do; in the Jewish tradition such acts are called *mitzvah*.

The kaddish is also recited by grievers during Sabbath services at the temple or synagogue and on special holy days like Yom Kippur or as part of a memorial service called Yizkor (Fox and Miller, 1992). I sat in a Sabbath service in a large synagogue when the rabbi asked those in grief to stand. I was stunned by the number of people who stood to join in reciting the kaddish. Each Sabbath there is something of a "time out" in the liturgy to recognize those who are in grief. In *Siddur Sim Shalom*, the book of worship used in Conservative Judaism, Mourner's Kaddish is prefaced with these words: "In love we remember those who no longer walk this earth. We are grateful to God for these lives, for the joys we shared, and for the cherished memories that never fade. May God grant to those who mourn the strength to see beyond their sorrow, sustaining them despite their grief. May the faith that binds us to our loved ones be a continuing source of comfort" (Rabbinical Assembly, 1998, p. 184).

As pastor-leader, you could use this prayer for closing the funeral/memorial service or the committal.

Teaching the kaddish to Christians

While I was leading a grief group in a very conservative congregation, one night a woman interrupted my lesson plan. "Excuse me. This is all well and good—but I can't pray anymore." We were not talking about prayer, but discussing Rando's choices for grievers. The griever persisted, "I can't pray. And when I come to church I can't sing, particularly those happy, snappy praise choruses." A chorus of "Me too" from others in the group supported her.

> A place in Heaven is reserved for those who weep but cannot pray.
> —Leo Rosten, 1977, p. 364

Some pastors would have responded, "What do you mean, 'You can't pray'? Just _____. You'll be praying again in no time."

"Are you willing to go outside your tradition to try prayer from another spiritual tradition?" I replied to the group. When they responded positively, I added, "Let me prepare some materials for our next meeting. The next week I passed out a sheet with the five paragraphs of the kaddish and asked participants to read the prayers silently and slowly. Then we read the kaddish aloud. "What is unusual in these prayers?" I asked.

"There is no mention of death," one griever noted. "Only God's goodness is mentioned," another added. "Correct. The focus of Jews in grief is on the goodness of God. You pray your way into a new way of thinking. Now, what hymns or praise choruses would convey the same message?" "Great Is Thy Faithfulness" and "Great Is the Lord" were suggested. I explained that many Christian grievers, without knowing it, sing the kaddish. At the end of the session, I asked them to read the kaddish each day for the next week.

I concede that I adapt generously from the kaddish. Some Jews rigorously insist that the kaddish cannot be prayed by individuals but only in the minyans. Besides, they argue, praying solo defeats the purpose of gathering the community. I answer the objection by saying that through this resource I have been able to give people who can no longer believe that God loves them—or that God is good—something they can hold on to on days where nothing makes sense to them. The kaddish is a hope seed for a spiritual future.

One way to familiarize your people with the kaddish is by teaching it in prayer meetings leading up to Thanksgiving or perhaps by using it as a responsive reading the Sunday before Memorial Day.

Thanksgiving or Memorial Day

Honest prayers. Death has a way of silencing even a prayer warrior. Not a few veteran saints have stated, "The heavens are as brass." One saint told me, "For a long time after my son's death, my prayers never got more than three feet above my bed." Brennan Manning pointedly addresses the difficulty: "When the shadow of Jesus' cross falls across our lives in the form of failure, rejection, abandonment, betrayal, unemployment, loneliness, depression, the loss of a loved one; when we are deaf to everything but the shriek of our own pain; when the world around us suddenly seems a hostile, menacing place—at those times we may cry out in anguish, "How could a loving God permit this to happen?" (2000, pp. 4-5).

Many grievers may not dare "cry out" such a statement, but they do think it. In those moments hell stands on tiptoes. Manning adds, "At such moments the seeds of distrust are sown. It requires heroic courage to trust in the love of God no matter what happens to us" (p. 5). Some grievers need someone to trust alongside them.

The pastor-leader gives people permission to pray honestly. Permission may be extended through modeling honesty in prayer.

The hymnal. The hymnal has been a prayer book for many Evangelicals. In mourning the loss of my mother, I often found myself singing her favorite songs, such as "Jesus Is All I Need" and "Jesus Will Walk with Me." I found such assurance in the words and from memories of sitting on a pew watching my mother sing (while I colored) and later sharing a hymnal and singing with her. My mother always let me know the songs she particularly liked by whispering, "That's a good one."

> *Jesus will walk with me.*
> *He will talk with me; He will walk with me.*
> *In joy or in sorrow, today and tomorrow,*
> *I know He will walk with me.*
> —Haldor Lillenas

At times I simply changed the lyrics to pray, "In joy or in sorrow, today and tomorrow, I know *You* will walk with me." In a sense, in congregational singing Christians rehearse the words of comfort they will eventually need. The absence of congregational singing during funerals in funeral homes adds to the sterile feel to many services. At my dad's funeral, because we sang, the funeral felt more as if my father were there. One of Wesley's great innovations was congregational singing at funerals. It's a practice we need to resume.

**It was not just to stall the inevitable that Jesus and
the disciples sang a hymn before they left the Last Supper—
it helped fortify Jesus for what was to come.**

Gospel songs such as "Just a Closer Walk with Thee" can be prayers. The pastor-leader hears out the lament, "I can't pray," and reminds the griever, "Can you sing? Maybe you're praying and don't know it."

**Wise pastor-leaders suggest, "Try
jump-starting prayer with a song."**

It's important to ask your members to pray for you. Robert LaFavre, after conducting more than 500 funerals, assesses the demands on a pastor:

Of the hours that a minister spends in the pulpit, at the desk, in his study, praying, visiting, counseling, planning, visionizing, and pouring oil on troubled waters, none can be perhaps more of a strain on his total being than his ministry at the time of death.

We pray for the family when death invades. But do we remember the pastor's need for prayer? Not only should you wrap your prayer arms around your pastor, but remember that he also could use a good, old-fashioned hug *(March 19, 1998, p. 3).*

Anoint

"Is any one of you sick? He should call the elders of the church to pray over him and anoint him with oil in the name of the Lord" (James 5:14). On the surface, some might fear that it is misusing Scripture to anoint the grieving. However, in some cultures, particularly the Hispanic, grief is considered an affliction. Thus, this text could read, "Is any one of you *afflicted or grieving?* Let the *griever* call for the elders of the church to pray over him." Pastors routinely assure grievers, "I will be praying for you, and the church will be praying." Congregations are urged, "Let's lift up so-and-so in prayer during this time of loss." Pastor-leaders go a step further to educate grieving parishioners to call for prayer and anointing in the name of the Lord.

Pastor-leaders pray deliberately, consistently, and creatively.

Many Christians consider anointing a special rite of the church, to be used occasionally. (After all, we have the most sophisticated medical system in the world—if you can afford it.) The Early Church had prayer and olive oil. Zach Thomas, in *Healing Touch: The Church's Forgotten Language,* explores the roots of this practice. When the elders showed up, they brought not a small vial of holy oil, as clergy use today, but rather a *bucket* of olive oil. By the time they had finished, you were soaked.

Something happens when grievers are prayed for.

Something happens when grievers are physically touched during prayer.

Something may happen when grievers are anointed.

> **We cannot pray the ache out of another, but we can bless it with the touch of our hands, the gift of our hug and our embrace. When we do this, we give the ache permission to go on its way.**
> —Joyce Rupp, 1988, p. 91

Why not anoint grievers at the conclusion of the funeral or memorial service (with their agreement)? This could be done in one of two ways. First, at the funeral or memorial service, ask those wishing to be anointed to come forward. Or instead of the common practice of shaking hands with grievers at the grave, anoint each one and make the sign of the Cross on the forehead in oil. The pastor-leader could quote from *The Book of Common Prayer* paraphrase of Ps. 51:12 when making the north-to-south motion, "Give me the joy of your saving help again" and on the east-to-west motion, "Sustain me with your bountiful Spirit."

Tradition says that these words were written after David's sin with Bathsheba *and* following the death of their seven-day-old unnamed son. Remind grievers and those in attendance that these words were framed by a grieving father and husband. These two petitions when used in a funeral or memorial service can become a griever's prayer.

Urge the griever to recall and recite these Psalm phrases whenever anxious, fearful, or overwhelmed:

> *Give me the joy of your saving help again.*
> *Sustain me with your bountiful Spirit.*

Pastor-leaders may also use a companion text such as "May the Lord bless *you* . . . and give *you* peace." If there are a number of grievers, alternate: May the Lord keep *you* . . . and make his face to shine upon *you*" or "May the peace of the Lord . . . go with *you*."

A pastor-leader could add to the benediction text, following the "in your going out and your coming in," these words: *in your grieving and in your healing.* This makes the blessing situation-specific, and it will be heard and remembered.

If the congregation recites Ps. 23, the anointing of the immediate mourners reinforces the psalmist, "You anoint my head with oil" (v. 5). By anointing we strengthen grievers.

Anointing can be done in the privacy of the home or in the moments traditionally spent with the family before the funeral service begins. But grief is a communal experience in the family of God. The church has long recognized that anointing is a public witness that may encourage others, in their moments, to seek and receive anointing also. On the morning of the Resurrection, the women went to the tomb to anoint the body of Jesus. We are just amending that example to anoint the bereaving.

Scripture

For some grievers, in the depth of loss, Scripture takes on a whole new meaning. Randy Sly discloses his practice of a grief-marked copy of the New Testament with Psalms and Proverbs. He explains, "My mind doesn't always track clearly during these times of stress, so certain scriptures are premarked that undergird the sense of hope and perspective that we can take with us" (1993, p. 18).

In sharing from the Psalms, you might pass on this observation from a wise rabbi: "There are no new kinds of tears: we cry the same tears as did David for his child" (David J. Wolpe, cited in Kay, 1993, p. 42).

The Psalms are punctuated with the tears of grievers. You will also want to mark John 14 and various passages of comfort from Paul.

Conclusion

Prayer is not the last resort. Prayer is the foundation resource in a pastor-leader's repertoire. Grief is a little less intrusive in the presence of prayer.

Goal of Pastoral Leadership

The pastor-leader prays. The pastor-leader supports the prayer efforts of grievers.

A Spiritual Formation Exercise

1. Go back and slowly read the kaddish. Circle any words or phrases that leaped out at you.
2. Now reread but pause after each section. Spend some time meditating on that fragment. Think of a hymn or chorus text that expresses the theme of this prayer. Sing it aloud. Consider changing the pronoun. For example, if you selected, "Great Is Thy Faithfulness," in the chorus change, "All I have needed Thy hand hath provided" to "All I have needed, *Lord, You* have provided."
3. Identify passages of Scripture to support each prayer.
4. Think about ways the kaddish could be used in a funeral: a responsive prayer, the framework for a solidly biblical funeral sermon.
5. Now put the ancient words of the kaddish in your own words. Write them out.

6. Ask God to give you understanding on how to use the kaddish with grievers in your care.

A Story That Will Preach

How many times have Christians sung the text "What a friend we have in Jesus" without hearing "all our sins *and griefs* to bear!" If anyone earned the right to compose these words, Joseph Scriven did. Born in Ireland, he intended to follow in his father's footsteps as a career naval officer. Poor health, however, made that dream impossible.

He migrated to England and fell in love. Tragically, his bride-to-be drowned the night before they were to be married. To escape this loss, he went to Canada, where he eventually fell in love with Eliza Roche. But she died suddenly in 1855 before they could marry. Out of his profound grief, Scriven wrote the poem that Charles Converse later set to music.

One day Scriven was ill, and a friend dropped by to look in on him. The friend happened to notice the handwritten poem on the table. As he read the words about a divine friendship he asked, "Did you write this?"

"Yes," Scriven answered. "The Lord and I did it between us."

Life never did get a lot better for this man. When his health failed, and with limited income, he became depressed. On October 10, 1886, residents of a little Canadian community named Bewdley found Scriven's body in the flume of a dam near Rice Lake. Although it was never determined whether the poet's death was an accident or suicide, Scriven was buried in an unmarked grave. However, the popularity of his lyrics prompted the community to erect a large marker to posthumously honor the man for the words that have brought comfort to so many.

In the days ahead, you, too, may feel that friends do not understand your grief. They *can't* understand your grief. Scriven's words speak to that feeling: "Can we find a friend so faithful / Who will all our sorrows share? / Jesus knows our ev'ry weakness; / Take it *[this grief]* to the Lord in prayer." *Pray.*

A Leadership Decision

As a result of reading this chapter,

1. _____

2. _____

> **Blessings as you journey with those who say good-bye.**
> **—Joyce Rupp to Harold Ivan Smith, signed in book**

9
Leading Through Ritualing

*Show me the manner in which a nation or a community cares
for its dead and I will measure with mathematical exactness
the tender mercies of its people, their respect for the
law of the land, and their loyalty to high ideals.*
—William Gladstone, 1938, p. 13

Key Point Summary
**Traditionally, family and friends were expected to attend
three rituals:**
- **the visitation or wake**
- **the funeral or memorial service**
- **the committal**

Rituals are a rite of passage and are "associated with a crisis or change in status" (Webster, 1983, p. 1018). Funeral rituals promote social, spiritual, and psychological reconciliation with change. C. S. Lewis insisted that rituals made griefs "more endurable" (cited in Wolfelt, 1994, p. 3). I would contend that rituals make loss more survivable and, according to Darcie Sims, "help connect, [and] become bridges between past, present, future or what was and what should be" (2000). In contemporary, fast-paced, "grief-lite" American culture, attendance at and participation in funeral rituals is being radically reexamined.

Increasingly with committals considered or identified in obituaries as private or "family only," many individuals consider participation as an either-or choice: Attend the visitation *or* attend the funeral/memorial service. One ritual, not both. Moreover, increasing numbers of families and friends are designing an alternative ritual celebration that may be both creative and chaotic, spiritual and nonreligious. Alternative rituals may be held during the traditional mourning ritual period (that is, immediately following a death) or delayed for weeks or months. John Welshons counsels, "Instead of overlooking this important life event, design one that is meaningful to you" (2000, p. 134). He goes on to suggest: "Feel free to be creative. Design your own rituals. . . . design unique ceremonies. Let your imagination run free. Let your family members' imaginations run free. Create rituals and ceremonies that will be inspirational, moving, meaningful, and healing . . . perhaps they might even be fun" (p. 155).

In some funeral rituals today, the pastor is relegated to serving as a master of ceremonies. The sermon or homily is not necessarily the "main event." That position goes to the givers of the eulogies.

The purposes for rituals

Something about death, possibly its permanence, motivates grievers to call for a minister to conduct a ritual. From long experience as a pastor, James M. Wall concludes, "We need the presence of others, we need the presence of God, to stand with us in grief" (1997, p. 819). And traditionally the person who can best facilitate that interaction so that the ordinary becomes extraordinary is a minister.

Many people are seemingly indifferent about religion but will want some sense of the spiritual in a funeral experience. York (2000) points out that in a postmodern age, a growing number of people want to limit or eliminate the traditional religious context of the service. Instead of a minister, they may turn to a trusted friend to lead the service. Increasingly in Germany, funerals are conducted under the leadership of *Redner* or "speakers" who conduct secular funerals (Downey, 1998, p. 358), some with a Christian flavor, because many German Protestant ministers are reluctant to conduct services for nonmembers.

Many grievers may not be sure what they believe at the moment—especially given the circumstances of the death—but they want a minister as a guide to help them begin to sort out the experience of loss. How the minister delivers "presence" is critical.

Indeed, through clear pastoral leadership as a representative of God, whether in a funeral home, cemetery, or at a scattering site, someone may well decide to "get acquainted with that God" whom the pastor has presented (Wilcock, 1996, p. 33) and represented. It is no wonder that the once-popular funeral hymn "Does Jesus Care?" resonates in the chorus, "O yes, He cares; I know He cares! / His heart is touched with my grief." However, it will be difficult for grievers to believe that Jesus cares if they see the pastor do a haphazard job. "OK. So Jesus cares—but do *you* care?"

Clearly, people have diverse understandings of what makes a ritual meaningful. Increasingly, one of the important roles of a pastor is to provide leadership in ritual design and performance. As I argue this, I keep in mind Kenneth L. Woodward's contention that "the funeral director has become by default a weaver of instant rituals" since "an increasing number of Americans confront death with no inherited faith or liturgy for support" (September 22, 1997, p. 62) or with no pastors active in their lives. Meaningful rituals are doorways to healing through which grievers walk (or crawl) (Wolfelt, 1994). On the other hand, poor ritual sabotages and complicates thorough healing.

Wolfelt notes that the American culture appears "to be forgetting" or at least, negating, the importance of ritual. Although humanity has created rituals to mark death since the beginning of time, Americans "seem to be rapidly moving toward the dominant Anglo-Saxon model of minimizing, avoiding and denying the need for rituals surrounding death" (p. 5). So true is this assessment that an early act of leadership with long-term implications may be to persuade the reluctant family to plan a ritual—even if their design does not correspond to other rituals you have performed or that the community recognizes as funeral ritual.

> **Meaningful funeral ceremonies are one of the most affirming means of helping our fellow human beings begin to embrace the pain and separation and loss after the death of someone loved.**
> —Alan Wolfelt, 1994, p. 3

The pastor-leader when told, "I don't like funerals" graciously responds, "Tell me what it is about funerals that you don't like. I may not like it either."

Two norms for grief expression

Tony Walter identifies two norms for expressing grief in Western societies: the *expressive* and the *reserved*.

The expressive. The expressive may be represented by the boisterous Irish wake and after-funeral gatherings as well as by the traditional African-American grief rituals. In the African-American community, the eulogy and the music are "typically designed to provoke the release of emotions" (Hines, 1991, p. 188). Many mourners feel free to give vent to their emotions openly; unrestrained grief is acceptable if not expected (Devore, 1990). Ronald Keith Barrett highlights differences in funeral ritual expectations on funeral ritual between lower socioeconomic and middle-class African-Americans. In the former, funeral services could generally be described as "emotional, traditional homegoing services" (1998, p. 90) in which the eulogist focuses on the particularness of the deceased and the congregation voices agreement with that assessment. Mourners expect a spirited service. However, middle- and upper-income African Americans—particularly professionals—increasingly prefer funerals that are clearly "less emotional, more stoic, and more formal" (p. 90) and more like traditional middle-class white funerals.

Friends from one socioeconomic level can be disappointed by the funeral rituals for a loved one from another economic level. After attending a workplace colleague's funeral, one friend complained: "It was cold to me—cut and dried. Not much was even said about my friend. I didn't feel as if I had even been to a funeral. In my church, when we have a funeral, you leave knowing you've been to a funeral and feeling that the deceased was somebody!"

The reserved. This form may be characterized as typical among mainline liturgical churches. In some faith traditions, funerals follow a highly prescribed ritual order, so that little variation exists between the funeral for Jane on Monday and the funeral for William on Thursday. Some friends and family find comfort in that predictable sameness. One pastor finds that this decreases the pressure on him. "When we don't know what to say, the book [*Book of Common Prayer, Book of Discipline, The Manual,* and so on] supplies the words. Wolfelt, however, challenges this "going by the book" mentality. "Without a eulogy and/or other personalized means of acknowledging this particular life and death," the result is "an empty, cookie-cutter formality" (1998, p. 46). In such predictable rituals ("been there, felt that") the participants can tune in and tune out, present but not actively participating.

The boundaries between reserved and expressive are not rigid. As any seasoned pastor knows, "members of the same family may hold different norms as to the proper way to grieve, causing rifts between members at a time when they most need to support each other" (Walter, 1999, p. 139). The question of who has the final power to make ritual plans can be hotly debated. Sometimes no matter what's decided, it's unacceptable to someone. Moreover, some family members may attempt to involve the pastor in encouraging or discouraging certain components. What is done or is not done can ruin the ritual for a participant.

Rifts over ritual can resurrect old family issues. Sometimes the pastor providing leadership in planning a ritual must navigate a minefield of issues that can be ignited with as simple a question as "Who will sit on the front row?" especially among people married more than once. Rifts arise when a person has migrated to a different faith tradition from the faith of origin. Imagine a predominantly Nazarene family sitting through a high-church Episcopalian funeral service. Imagine the predominantly Episcopal family and friends sitting through the comparatively informal Nazarene service. Nelsen (1998) recalls, "The family fought at the church over whether Kathy should be buried with a rosary in her hands, although she had converted to Lutheranism many years earlier and the service was taking place at her Lutheran church."

The dispute, however, did not end in the arrangements conference. "The disagreement spilled over into the parking lot with various family members making obscene hand gestures at each other from the mortuary limousine. Suddenly, the rigid Victorian code of funeral etiquette practiced by Southern Blacks made elegant sense. It enforces civility at this most stressful time" (Nelsen, 1998, p. 29).

One funeral director told me that he often longs to wear a referee's shirt under his dark suit. "If only I could give penalties," he said, smiling. "Some folks will be on good behavior until the rituals are completed; then, watch out! But if they have been drinking, all bets are off!" Uncivil incidents are remembered long after the pastor's remarks have been forgotten.

During the mourning period (from death to burial), the mourners are "betwixt and between" (Turner, 1977, cited in Walter, 1999, p. 28). The dead, although not alive, are not yet firmly anchored with the dead; the mourners are also between statuses. Thus, funeral rites "transport the deceased to the land of the dead and the bereaved back to the land of the living" (Walter, 1999, p. 28).

The ritual, particularly among people of a shared faith, is a witness of that transfer and a promise: Just as we supported you in this ritual, we will support you in the unfolding transition in the days ahead. In one sense, we may sing, "God will take care of you" but in essence we are singing, "*We* will take care of you."

According to social theorist Arnold van Gennep, rituals are necessary to move both the living and the dead through the transitional into the permanent. Rituals are a means to accomplish one of the essential tasks of grief: to relocate the dead (cited in Worden, 1991, p. 16).

I was stunned in one funeral, after the opening Scripture from the Gospel of John, to hear the unmistakable voice of Ray Stevens bellowing, "Everything is beautiful in its own way" (on tape). Later, after hearing the "replay" of the arrangements conference, I understood how the song had been selected. Concession and compromise led to a request: "Can we all get along on this?" One director told me he regularly says, "This sounds like a family issue. I will step out into the hall. When you've settled it, I'll come back."

When rituals are not held, mourners are left, in Walter's words, "adrift and alone." Indeed, for some, rituals will be in interactions with clinicians. Sometimes, as I have learned in my work in a hospital setting, a "left-out" griever needs a reritual or a "ritual for one." It should be noted that many grievers are so numb that they are passive experiencers of even the most poignant ritual.

> **Meaningful funerals do not just happen. They are well-thought-out rituals that, at least for a day or two, demand your focus and your time. But the planning needn't be a burden if you keep in mind that the energy you expend . . . will help you and other mourners in your grief journeys for years to come.**
> **—Alan Wolfelt, 1995, October 26**

**The funeral liturgy can be a life raft that
gets grievers to a secure, safe place.**

Cultural deritualization of funeral traditions

For many funeral-goers and funeral planners, the traditional funeral has lost its value. Many prefer ritual "lite." Others want a ritual smorgasbord. Some are, no doubt, influenced by the creativity and innovation common in weddings. Wolfelt recognizes several factors in deritualization.

1. We live in the world's first death-free generation. Howard Raether charges that American society is both death-defying and death-denying. "Millions of young people have never experienced a death and a funeral" (1998, p. 82) other than in a movie. Yet in a few years they will find themselves—as pastors or as grievers—planning something they have never attended.

A pastor-leader becomes something of a salesman to convince the mourner(s), "This is something you need, and here are some options for you to think about." Jack Bauer, a veteran funeral director, suggests that funeral directors "have to take the lead in creating new types of services for families that do not want a traditional funeral" (cited in Wolfelt, 2000, p. 18). What about the family who says at the start,

> If you are 40 or older and have never attended a truly meaningful funeral, you probably don't realize the importance of having one.
> —Alan Wolfelt, 1994, fall, p. 4

"We want direct cremation—no rituals!" Bauer, again from long experience, adds, "Many families that request direct cremation really *do* want a service if we educate them about all of the different choices they have" (p. 20). So the pastor also needs to be an educator.

2. We live in a mobile, fast-paced culture. Our family and friends may be scattered across the country. In the late 1880s and early 1900s, many people walked to funerals or rode a streetcar. Now funeral rituals have to be coordinated with airline schedules, family calendars, and traffic flow patterns. It is no longer unusual to find these words at the end of an obituary: "Services will be held at a later date." Some families never get around to doing a ritual.

3. Americans value self-reliance. Some are reluctant to inconvenience anyone. Sometimes all it takes is one "in denial" family member to suggest delaying the service, especially if the body has been cremated. In a culture that values do-it-yourself-and-save jobs, why not eliminate the pastor?

4. We discount the traditional, particularly if it is linked with faith. Admittedly, some individuals have had negative experiences at fu-

nerals. Trillin (1993) comments that with
his experience with funeral rituals, you
can expect some grumbling afterward.

> **It must be natural for people feeling a loss to fasten on some factual error in a eulogy or some way that the setting or the order of service was inappropriate.**
> —Calvin Trillin, 1993, p. 27

   Trillin describes riding in the car after
services for a Yale University friend and listening to the complaints such as "I wasn't
interested in hearing them read passages
from the King James Version. I wanted to
hear what they [the ministers] had to say
about Mike" (1993, p. 28). Another fumed,
"The departed could have been a stockbro-
ker" rather than a well-known Maine humorist. That talent was not even
acknowledged in the long service.

   "Even as we grumbled, though, I acknowledged that Mike, who was
an eccentric but not a rebel, had a traditionalist side that would have
been horrified at any thing other than a proper Episcopalian funeral."

   Trillin concludes, "I suppose it was simply more convenient to be angry at the service than at the hit-and-run driver, who had eluded the police and would always elude us" (pp. 28-29). Thus, pastor-leaders will
naturally get blamed for things that were not their responsibility.

   5. Americans have jettisoned the symbols of death. Symbols
are resources that by their very dynamism make individuals think about,
imagine, and get into contact with another deeper reality (Arbuckle,
2000, p. 122). Americans seem to be afraid
of grief symbols. No one wears a "mourning coat" to a ritual; no funeral wreaths
hang on the front door of the residence of
the deceased. Many do not wear black to
funerals. I have been surprised in death
notices to read, "No black, please" or "No
ties, please." Many adults these days do
not feel a need to dress up for a funeral.
Maybe I'm old-fashioned, but I can't be-

> **As you are, so once was I. As I am, so you shall be. Prepare for death and follow me.**
> —Common North American tombstone epitaph

lieve that shorts, T-shirts, and baseball caps are appropriate for a funeral.
Wolfelt says that the absent symbol is the body and casket. Thus, eliminating the symbols is linked to eliminating the rituals. Casual dress is a
way to deny the seriousness of what is taking place.

   6. Americans deny their own mortality. Rituals psychologically
function like mirrors: Someone is next. Could that someone be *you*?

   Death may not be optional, but rituals increasingly are. Avoiding rituals is a way adults deny their own mortality. Many people are so good at
multitasking that they are physically present at rituals but emotionally
absent. Many pastors find funeral crowds to be a tough audience.

Objections to rituals

If you have pastored long, you know the variety of ways people object to particular items included in the funeral. They may not directly say, "What's the point of that?" but the question can be subtly communicated with a raised eyebrow or a look. Any opposition may be enough to cancel that element. Therese Rando has identified these purposes for funeral rituals:

- Confirm and reinforce the reality of death
- Assist in the acknowledgment and expression of feelings of loss
- Offer the survivors a vehicle for expressing their feelings
- Stimulate the recollection of the deceased
- Assist mourners in beginning to accommodate the changed relationship between themselves and the deceased [and between themselves and members of the family and support network]
- Allow for input from the community and help mourners form an integrated image of the deceased (1984, pp. 180-82)

Michael Zedek also identifies the value of funeral rituals:

- To help us acknowledge what has happened
- To help us know what we are when something has happened to us
- To help us proceed when such a thing has happened (1999)

Thus, ritual helps grievers "act our way into right thinking" and right response. Through planning, preparing for, and implementing rituals for grievers, ministers help grievers make the service special. Some are like former United States Senator Barry Goldwater, who decided to have a funeral ritual for himself only after attending a "good" funeral for a friend. The pastor-leader evaluates the assessment not only of "church folk" and family but also that of the spiritual strangers who attended the ritual.

Big changes in the works

1. **More people are taking ownership of their funeral rituals.** Historically before the Reformation, funeral rituals were exclusively the responsibility of the pastor. A pastor's authority and leadership were typically unquestioned. When challenged, the pastor prevailed. Then, during the Reformation, the role of the clergy was de-emphasized as funerals came to be

---

The Primary Issues to Be Weighed by a Pastor

- The worship nature of the ritual
- The personal needs of the individuals involved in relationship to those of the corporate fellowship of believers and
- The responsibility to give leadership and exert authority at these times, in fulfilling their prophetic, teaching and pastoring roles

—Don Hustad, 1981, p. 213

considered civil experiences. The most one could hope for was that the pastor would attend and might offer a prayer. The seedling of de-emphasizing pastoral leadership had been planted (Niebergall and Lathrop, 1986). During the Reformation the role of the pastor was reassessed (McLean, 1996; Dugan, 1996). In the postmodern world, the seedlings sprouted.

As the mortician (one who prepared the body) became the undertaker or one who "undertook" all the physical necessities—embalming, building a casket, transporting the body, supplying chairs, and so on, the pastor was still very much in charge, particularly of the funeral and committal—simply because the funeral was held in *his* church, and the burial was often held in *his* cemetery. No one ever had to ask, "Who's in charge here?"

For several decades, the pastor shared leadership with the undertaker; boundaries were respected, particularly when these professionals were friends. In some cases, the personalities of the two men, long pastorates, and long service in the community made that relationship predictable. Today, many pastors have excellent collegial relationships with funeral directors; more than one director has said to a pastor, "How do *you* want to handle this?"

Yet, as more funerals were held in funeral home chapels rather than in churches, and the dead were buried in privately owned or municipally owned cemeteries, the pastor's authority began to wane. These days, in some cases, the pastor's leadership is purely persuasive. The funeral director tells the pastor what is expected of him. In some cases, the pastor is a "hired hand" for the funeral.

Lots of pastors ran funerals from a managerial position. Thus, it was either "my way or the highway." No few pastors dug in their heels and said, "Not in my church you won't!" The next time a family member died, the funeral was held in the funeral home chapel.

James Hudnut-Beuller comments on the quiet change taking place in funeral rituals: "People are taking greater control of their own funerals, and they are by extension no longer allowing pastors and priests and rabbis to have exclusive control of what goes on" (cited in Breslin, 1998, p. 3). Wolfelt adds that an increasing number of families are now requesting that funeral services be held in other locations than funeral chapels or churches.

> **Almost any location that holds a special meaning for the family and friends of the person who died is appropriate.**
> —Jack Bauer in Alan Wolfelt, 2000, p. 18

"While this is often particularly appropriate for non-religious families, even deeply religious services can be held in atypical locations if the family and the funeral officiant are so inclined" (2000, p. 18). He reports on funerals held in a country club, an ice-skating rink, and a tennis court and cautions funeral directors, "You will hold services in a variety of settings in the future" (p. 18), a prediction that pastors also must consider.

Some families will stretch the "almost any location." Bauer advises funeral director colleagues that they must be open to facilitating rituals anywhere the family chooses. "Funerals always require organization and dignity, but beyond that, the sky is the limit" (p. 20). For some pastors, faith-based rituals in some locations will be difficult to accommodate.

2. Funerals are events. One distraught mother coming out of a funeral was asked by another person, "Well, how did it compare with your son's funeral?" The woman felt as if she had been physically struck. She mumbled an answer and rushed away but later wrote "Miss Manners" (Judith Martin) for guidance. (Increasingly the advice columnists are the arbitrators of funeral etiquette.) Miss Manners (1999, April 18) replied, "Miss Manners was already aware that everyone in modern society had become a movie critic, rating all aspects of life for style and entertainment value. She just hadn't imagined that it had gone so far that a mother would be asked to rate her son's memorial service against what apparently should be considered competition."

3. Bad rituals prejudice against any rituals. Every pastor and funeral director has heard stories about "bad" funerals—funerals that leave both saying, "You've got to be kidding me." Ellen Dissanayake, a cultural anthropologist who studies ceremonies and ritual, does not mince words: "Today's 'traditional' ceremonies are frequently deplorable" (Dissanayake, 1995, p. 139). Nonreligious friends can be annoyed by a ritual imposed upon them. Dissanayake describes feeling alienated at a close friend's funeral by "the bland impersonal remarks of a stranger and the irrelevant hymn we were asked to sing" (p. 139). She questions how such a ritual could be helpful: "I felt a sudden pang of loss, wanting to tell my dead friend about the meaninglessness of the stupid funeral I had just attended" (p. 139).

4. Leadership says you "could" do this and only sparingly uses the S word: should. The pastor-leader persuades, never browbeats. After all, the pastor knows that he or she can win the liturgical battle and lose the war (relationship with family members). One family contrasted the style between two pastors. For the first funeral (planning a parent's funeral), the pastor resisted the family's suggestions, saying, "I'm not sure you want to do that" or "That probably won't be possible." When the second parent died, another pastor demonstrated leadership as he responded to requests, "Let's see if we can make that happen." The first pastor was a manager; the second was a pastor-leader.

After a good ritual, the friends and family still grieve, but in Henry Coffin's analogy, the loss "is a clean wound" (1997, p. 346).

Goal of Pastoral Leadership

The goal is not merely to "do" a funeral ritual. The goal is to lead an assembled congregation—probably never to be together again—in a ritual that celebrates the life of the deceased and the life of Jesus Christ.

A Story That Will Preach

In many ways it's never too late to have a ritual. Michael Mayne knows that and made ritual an important part of his ministry as he rose through ecclesiastical ranks to become the dean of Westminister Abbey, where he presided over rituals for many of England's leaders. Mayne's understanding of the need for ritual was rooted in an incident in his boyhood—actually an absence of ritual. His father, the rector of a small Anglican parish, on a Saturday afternoon wrote a note to Mayne's mother, climbed the tower of the church, and threw himself to the floor below. At the time, Michael was three years old. In those days, the church allowed no marked grave or memorial for a person who committed suicide. Now Mayne's mother was penniless, and the family was homeless. The shame of the act was captured in the words of the coroner at the inquest: "I cannot conceive of a clergyman desecrating holy ground . . . unless his mind was very much deranged." So after a cremation, Mayne's father's ashes "were scattered to the four winds, and nobody spoke of him again."

Sixty years passed. Mayne notes, "Life comes full circle in the most unpredictable of ways, and there is a kind of healing." A few elderly parishioners talked to their rector and argued that there should be some memorial for Mayne's father's five years of service. After all, times had changed; the church now viewed suicide quite differently. (And that orphan boy had become one of England's leading preachers.) So on a hot August day, on Mayne's mother's 94th birthday, children, grandchildren, and great-grandchildren returned to that small church for a simple service in which a stone honoring his father was finally placed in the chancel wall.

In those moments, standing by the pulpit in which the father he could not remember had preached, Mayne concluded, "Even in the worse of events, God is present, and there are possibilities of redemption" (1998, p. 58). (A pastor-leader knows those words to be true.) An elderly parishioner handed one grandson a photocopy of the newspaper story covering the death. Through that gift, Mayne finally learned many of the details of his father's death.

It's never too late for a ritual. But at times,

the wisest choice is to make room for a ritual in our lives now.

Death robs us of so much—let it not rob us of ritual.

A Spiritual Formation Exercise

Spend time with Acts 5:1-11.

1. Write Mayne's words on a sheet of paper. Spend time pondering them: "Even in the worse of events, God is present, and there are possibilities of redemption."
2. What is the bridge between the narrative of the absence of ritual in this biblical account and Mayne's narrative?
3. Reread verse 11: "Great fear seized the whole church and all who heard about these events." Think about the story of Michael Mayne's father, and consider the "all" who possibly heard about the suicide of Rector Mayne. What did they hear "about these events"? How could a ritual have made a difference in the lives of those who made up the "all," especially in a three-year-old's life?
4. Can you recall a funeral that created fear in you? in your "whole church"? How as a pastor did you lead a ritual in such difficult circumstances? How did God help you? How would you lead that ritual now?
5. Finally, take a moment and reflect on the words of James M. Wall that a ritual is a way of acknowledging, "We need the presence of others, we need the presence of God, to stand with us in grief" (1997, p. 819).
6. Spend moments in prayer asking God to give you more awareness of the opportunities for providing leadership through ritual.

A Leadership Decision

As a result of reading this chapter, I want to

1. _____

2. _____

Making special is a fundamental human proclivity or need. We prepare special meals and wear special garb for important occasions. We find special ways of saying important things. Ritual and ceremony are occasions during which everyday life is shaped and embellished to become more than ordinary.

—Ellen Dissanayake, 1995, p. 223

10

Officiating the Visitation, Funeral, and Committal

*The last thing you would want is to have a "boring" funeral,
and the best thing one can say about a "successful"
Irish wake is that the deceased would have really enjoyed it.*
—Monica McGoldrick, 1991, p. 180

In previous times, viewing the corpse was a required means of confronting the reality of the death. Remember Jesus' question, "Where have you laid him?" and Mary and Martha's answer, "Come and see, Lord" (John 11:34). The viewing was a way to make certain with one's own eyes that the individual had died.

The goal was that through community and church support, the estate (in the days before women could own property in their own name) was redistributed. The community expressed some degree of responsibility for the emerging restructuring of the family so survivors could "survive." In an era before Social Security, life insurance, and pensions, economic survival was foremost. Many widows remarried or turned their homes into boardinghouses while others entered prostitution in order to survive. In cultures that practiced primogeniture, everything was transferred to the oldest son, which, given the reality of sibling rivalry, created great dysfunction. Catherine Clinton points out that in antebellum South, following the death of the plantation owner, the wife (mother) lost her place as "mistress" of the plantation to the daughter-in-law. Until recent times, a death often translated into economic upheaval.

> **Historic Purposes of Rituals**
> * **To ensure that the dead were, in fact, dead**
> * **To ensure that they stayed dead**
> * **To "carry the members of the family through their dealings with grief"**
>   —Charles Hatchett, 1995, p. 477

The viewing

Viewings were originally held in the residence of the deceased. However, with growing urbanization and the popularity of apartments for city dwellers, there was inadequate space to accommodate a viewing. This led to the development in the 1880s of the funeral "home" with a rentable parlor, which not only provided space but also preserved the privacy of the family residence from intrusion, particularly by individuals on the fringe of the social network. By shifting the visitation (viewing or calling hours as the practice is called in some areas) to the funeral home, the family's interaction with the public was both curtailed and supervised. (This was another step in both the growing privatizing of death and transfer of leadership away from the family and the pastor to the funeral director.) That the director posted "hours" and discouraged the around-the-clock wake further controlled the event.

Traditionally people did not just "drop in" at a visitation for a few moments. Friends came for the duration (or a significant portion) of the wake, even on successive nights; in fact, some spent the night sitting up with the body, even at the funeral home.

The visitation was conversation-focused and encouraged talking not only with the family but also with others who came to pay their respects.

The funeral was liturgy or ritual focused. Opportunities for conversation with the chief mourners (the family) were limited.

Over time in urban areas, the formal viewing became a sanctioned way for people from different social circles to interact: "How did *you* know Mary?" Thus, friends from Little League could meet friends from the workplace; friends from the church could meet friends from a bowling league. In small communities these friendships overlap, but not necessarily in large urban areas. In fact, the visitation gives the family a setting in which to meet intimate strangers with whom the loved one spent significant amounts of time: "So you're Tom. He talked about you so much. It's good to meet you finally."

Accompanying greeters

No one should have to go through dying, death, and bereavement alone. That concept is universal, but particularly so among people of faith. If John Donne was correct in saying, "No man is an island," a community is affected, to some degree, by any death.

This concept of companioning is part of all religious traditions. However, different religions and cultures define caring in diverse ways. For example, when a Buddhist dies, the number of rituals will be determined by the particular Buddhist tradition practiced by the deceased (Japanese Buddhists one service; Ceylon or Cambodian tradition up to three funerals).

Christians trace funeral ritual observance back to the Jewish heritage.

Arthur Green notes that *levayah,* the Hebrew word for funeral, literally translates "accompaniment" (1999, p. 242). People of the Jewish faith have historically believed that the deceased and their family should be accompanied to the final resting place. Joseph asked Pharaoh for permission to bury his dead father properly (Gen.

> The time immediately following death is often one of bewilderment and may involve shock or heartrending grief for the family and close friends. The ministry of the Church at this time is one of gently accompanying the mourners in their initial adjustment to the fact of death and the sorrow this entails.
> —The International Commission on English in the Liturgy, 1990, p. 21

50:4-5), a request that led to a lavish processional ("All Pharaoh's officials accompanied him—the dignitaries of the court and all the dignitaries of Egypt" [v. 7]). For those who died without family, friends, or means, burial became a *mitzvah,* a religious obligation or responsibility (Van Beck, 2000).

The first hours following a death make up what Elizabeth A. Johnson labels "the great darkness of grief" (1999, p. 9). Through snatches of conversation, stories, hugs, familiar faces, and tears, friends and neighbors communicate to grievers, *You are not alone. You are not going to be abandoned.* After sudden deaths, in spite of repeated denials and the *I just can't believe it!* expressions, the visitation offers the extended social network, as well as the family, a chance to confront communally the reality of this death and to begin to anticipate the consequences.

The early Christian community abandoned the religious tradition (Num. 19:11-22) that contended that the presence of a corpse "brought defilement to the house" (Smith and Cheetham, 1875, p. 253) and to anyone who touched it.

In the days before embalming and preservation, burial had to be reasonably immediate, particularly in hot, dry climates, often within 24 hours for most persons of Jewish faith, although never on the Sabbath or holy days (Magida, 1996). This immediacy is illustrated in one of the earliest descriptions of pallbear-

> For Christians, the deceased was not a ghoul to be feared nor an evil spirit to be warded off, but a saint to be respected, honored, loved, and accompanied with psalms, hymns, and prayers the last steps of the way (in the earliest Christian funerals, even given the kiss of peace). The dead body was [not] a mere shell to be discarded as rubbish.
> —Thomas Long, 1999, p. 506

ers found in Acts 5. When Ananias lied to the elders, he was struck dead.

"Then the young men came forward, wrapped up his body, and carried him out and buried him" (v. 6) apparently without the knowledge of Sapphira, his wife (v. 7). Three hours later, after she also lied and died, bearers repeated the process. Eventually, because the Early Church so valued friendship, the early Christians began delaying burial so that friends might

- "come and weep and take their last look" (Basilios, 1991, p. 425)
- extend condolences to the family and to those who made up "the household of faith" (Gal. 6:10, KJV) and
- witness the promises of future assistance

> For mourners, an invitation to see the body is an invitation to say goodbye and to touch someone they love for the last time. It is also an invitation to confront their disbelief that someone they deeply cared for is gone and cannot return. Far from being morbid, open-caskets help acknowledge the reality of death and the transition from life before the loss to life after.
> —Alan D. Wolfelt, 1998, June, p. 20

Little wonder that James prodded the Early Church leadership, "Religion that God our Father accepts as pure and faultless is this: to look after widows and orphans in their distress and to keep oneself from being polluted by the world" (1:27). In some segments of Christianity, there has been a tendency to insert ellipsis marks between "this" and "to keep oneself." Worldliness and its evils have been more an element of concern than the care of widows and orphans.

Alan D. Wolfelt does not see the visitation as some relic of funeral tradition but points to the need for a visitation not just for the immediate family members but also for friends, neighbors, colleagues, and fellow communicants of a community of faith (1998, June). Rarely is the phrase "See how they love one another" more moving than at a time of death.

Contemporary trends and the visitation

The visitation is still an important ritual of leave-taking. The visitation is important for

- those who cannot attend a funeral/memorial service because of work or family commitments
- those who dislike large crowds
- those who dislike funerals/memorial services
- those who are time-structured (they determine the amount of time spent at a visitation—it's difficult to leave a funeral "early")
- those who wish to interact with the family (Eakes, 1990) or others in an extended social network. Indeed, for some, the visitation takes on a reunion setting: "I haven't seen you since . . ."

However, two contemporary trends work against traditional visitation

- The growing acceptance of cremation (25 percent in 1999 national-ly and growing) (Walczak, 2000, p. 27) eliminates a body to view (although some families now opt for a limited viewing before the cremation; caskets may, in fact, be rented).
- The busy pace of this culture does not make it easy to add some-thing to an already overpacked schedule.

Suppose a work colleague dies. Given the size of metropolitan com-munities, he or she might live a considerable distance from a coworker (even be halfway across the country or world). Getting to and from the visitation adds to the time expense. Child care must also be taken into consideration (given the number of individuals who believe a funeral home is not child-friendly). Who has time to attend all the rituals espe-cially in a metropolitan area? Moreover, in a high-pressured workplace, time off for a funeral is not always easily arranged. As one supervisor suggested to an employee, "Can't you just drop in at the visitation?" (that is, on the employee's personal time).

Some families fear that if they choose traditional rituals, few will at-tend. Many families, until a visitation or funeral, are completely unaware of the extent of the social network of a family member.

The combination visitation and funeral

One response to time demands is to combine the visitation *and* funer-al. The visitation takes place prior to the funeral service for one or two hours (or 30 minutes according to one death notice in the *Kansas City Star*). Other families elect for a reception after the memorial service.

Moreover, some arbiters of etiquette do not value the visitation.

According to Emily Post, "The visit to the funeral home need not last more than five or ten minutes. As soon as the visitor has expressed his sympathy to each member of the family, and spoken a moment or two with those he knows well, he may leave" (1992, p. 549).

Five or 10 minutes? Such a casual attitude toward a visitation would have been considered outrageous by our parents or grandparents. Not surprisingly, some conclude, "Why bother going?" Others take a drop-in approach to visitations—one more thing on a day's agenda to get done.

In reality, these days many people ask themselves, "How well did I know this individual? Well enough to be inconvenienced?"

An experience that enhanced appreciation

I was convinced anew of the value of the visitation when my mother died. At first, considering my mother's age and the depletion of her social network over the years, I second-guessed my siblings' decision to have two nights of visitation. But I was surprised by the turnout and thoroughly enjoyed the chance to visit with old friends, extended family members, neighbors, and members of my mother's church. I especially appreciated the stories people told about my mother.

> **Visitations have a vital but informal role to play in ritualing the dead and in providing support to the living.**

Funerals and memorial services

Funerals for Protestants were once commonly held in the home of the deceased but might be held in a church if a large crowd was expected or if the deceased was a leader in a congregation. Eventually, funeral homes added chapels for the convenience of families and those who did not have a church affiliation and to make it easier for Catholics to attend funerals of Protestant friends (and vice versa). In a church, funerals were clearly an act of worship (Blair, 1998, p. 28). White insists, "The Christian funeral is worship above all else, not primarily grief therapy" (1990, p. 297).

> The presence and participation of the dead human body at its funeral is, as my father told it, every bit as important as the bride's being at her wedding, the baby at its baptism.
>
> —Thomas Lynch, 1997, p. 24

Admittedly, this culture values convenience. Robert C. Anderson is rather direct: "Funerals at mortuary chapels are more convenient for the funeral director" (1985, p. 25) but also solidify the director's authority or leadership, since the service is on his or her turf rather than the pastor's turf. However, that process of the transfer of site of ritual, which has long been held significant, "deprives the family of a significant gathering in the more natural environment of the meeting place of the church" (p. 259).

Do people baptize babies at the hospital or the church? Do brides marry in a marriage chapel or in a church? Why, then, do we shift this ritual to a neutral setting that in essence must be rented?

Anderson states, "The funeral chapel is an unnatural place, signifying that death is an unnatural occurrence. But in the life of a Christian many significant, natural occasions of life occur within the church building. It is fitting, therefore, that the final event may take place there as well" (1985, p. 259).

Why? Anderson argues that most people feel more comfortable in a church; the music instruments commonly used are there so that a congregation "feels greater freedom to sing and worship in surroundings that are familiar" (p. 260). There is something of a vicious cycle created by the fact that funerals are sad; if there is congregational singing in the funeral home setting, it is awkward. Why? Because the service is being held in a setting designed more for optimally viewing the corpse rather than for worshiping God!

Many pastors believe that we contribute to the awkwardness of a funeral by scheduling it in a place that is discomforting for many, distressing for some. Roman Catholic leadership has been resistant to moving the funeral from a church setting to a funeral home.

The Christian shaping of funeral rituals

Christians were particularly influential in shaping the funeral as something of a witness to their belief in eternity and as a protest against prevailing Roman culture:

- The deceased, if faithful, was considered a victor, and the procession was modeled after a general's triumphant return from war. A martyr or leader's body was carried on a stretcher "with the head raised and exposed" (Rush, 1969, p. 895) for all to see.
- The procession occurred in the daytime as contrasted with pagan funeral rituals that were held at night. In fact, the word "funeral" comes from the Latin *funeralis,* or "torchlight procession."
- Third, early Christians rejected "the noisy exhibitions of grief" (Stannard, 1975, p. 99) typical of that day's funerals and limited the number of participants.

Originally the corpse was carried from the residence to the place of burial. With the development of church buildings, Christians instituted a service at a church as an intermediate destination.

The influence of the Reformation

The Reformation prompted major change in all rituals, but particularly the funeral and postfuneral acts, such as praying for the dead. Martin Luther vigorously condemned vigils, masses for the dead, processions, belief in purgatory, and all other "hocus-pocus on behalf of the dead" as "popish abominations" (Dugan, 1996, p. 151). In many areas of 17th-century Germany, for a period, Protestants had no funerals; some Lutherans were "content simply to sing hymns at the burial" (Niebergall and Lathrop, 1986, p. 125).

In time, some Puritans came to regard the funeral as a secular matter and had no services; others created brief services with psalms, scripture, and a brief prayer (White, 1990, p. 291). Significant innovation came with John and Charles Wesley and the Methodists, whose tradition of "singing funerals" began in 1775 when John Nelson, a friend of the Wesley brothers, died. Nelson's friend William Shent began calling out hymns, and mourners sang during the procession to the grave. The early Methodist funerals were marked by joy (George, 1986), and Charles Wesley's song texts about death such as "Come let us join friends above" were often sung to popular bar tunes.

Location of rituals

Today, in sprawling urban settings, time is money. The funeral procession can be a logistical nightmare in many urban areas. Why take so much time to transfer the body to a church for the funeral, especially if the family wants a brief service? While White prefers that funerals be held in churches, a position shared by many pastors, Robert Blair offers a different perspective:

> I know of no spiritual reason why they [funerals] should be held in church sanctuaries, but I can think of many practical reasons for conducting them in mortuary chapels, especially in urban areas. It can be hazardous to drive in long processions through the streets of large cities from the service to the burial place. The mortuary facilities are usually better suited for funeral arrangements than are church buildings. However, it is good to accommodate any family that prefers to use the church building *(1998, p. 23).*

Moreover, given the distance people drive from a residence to a church, particularly if they attend a megachurch, a funeral home might be closer to the residence and the cemetery. For some the decision is convenience and economy. Having the service at the funeral home eliminates transfer expense and saves time and eliminates another portion of the funeral procession.

A psychological factor may also prove influential on the location of service decision. Many individuals are warned, "If you have the service for your loved one in the church, then every time you go to church you'll be reminded of it."

Purpose

Why have a funeral? More people these days ask that question. Alan D. Wolfelt charges that America "as a culture appears to be forgetting the importance of the funeral ritual" (1994, p. 5) and seems to be heading toward minimizing, avoiding, or denying the need for public rituals. Even some pastors believe that the funeral with a body's presence is archaic and morbid.

Direct disposal

In an efficiency culture, we've seen a startling increase in what's termed "direct disposal," which means no viewing, no service, and immediate cremation or a brief, private "family only" graveside service or scattering. Wolfelt (1994, October) noted that many who say, "When I die, don't go to any trouble," translates into a family's decision, "OK—we won't" (p. 54). In obituaries published in the *Kansas City Star* and other newspapers it is not unusual to read, "At the request of the deceased, no services or visitation have been scheduled."

James F. White (1990) offered two theological reasons for questioning direct disposals. Funerals are a ritual vehicle to console the bereaved and formally commend the deceased to God.

Purposes of funerals

Robert Blair identifies three reasons for the funeral ritual: to help mourners confront the death's reality; to support them as they come to terms with the loss; and to confront all with God's love and His claim on our lives (1998, p. 62).

I think there is a societal need for a pause in the rhythms of life to say a public good-bye.

> **The religious funeral offers a body of believers the chance to participate corporately in the good-bye process.**

Some argue that the body needs to be present in order to "help confront the reality of death." Other Christians firmly protest such a conclusion: "I want to remember him as he was." Many Christian leaders have been influenced by Jessica Mitford's seminal book *The American Way of Death* and its stinging critique of the funeral "industry" as reason enough, particularly the attempt by morticians to "pretty up" death with embalming, cosmetics, and lighting with an underlying desired goal of a mourner's murmur: "He looks just like he's sleeping." Many believers would argue that such attempts to debrutalize death are counterproductive.

Disposal of the body

One reality is that the body of the deceased has to be properly disposed of. With embalming, depending on the conditions of the body at the time of death, a funeral may be delayed for as long as a week. By contrast, without embalming, that window is about 24 hours. When the body is quickly disposed of, a memorial service can be held anytime in the future—a fact increasingly recognized by time-conscious people.

Some funeral directors, ministers, and clinicians find that those who opted for direct disposal may have difficulty reconciling with the death. One funeral director had clients who wanted direct cremation when their mother died (no visitation, no memorial service). However, a year later, when their father died, they approached the funeral director. "What we did [or didn't do] when Mom died wasn't right. What shall we do for Dad?" They chose a traditional funeral. However, an interesting thing happened at the cemetery for the committal of the father/grandfather's cremains. A grandson asked, "OK, I see where Grandpa is—now where's Grandma?" (McCormick, 2000, May, p. 23). "So, a nine-year old educated three college professors about the value of a traditional funeral service. We use this example when we talk to people. . . . I think it is where people are today—we don't want to stop our lives and take the time to say goodbye" (Pat Sefton, cited in McCormick, p. 23).

In every decision relating to funeral ritual, it's good to ask, "Yes, but is it good for everyone, including the children?"

The memorial service

A memorial service without the body or the cremains present is an alternative ritual preferred by many families. Among the factors influencing the increase in memorial services are the following:

- With no body to be buried and the ritual not being governed by transportation factors or cemetery hours, the service can be scheduled days, weeks, months after the death (and in reality, in some families that translates "at a more convenient time" or, in wording that commonly appears in obituaries, "to be announced at a later date").
- Because there is no body to be taken to a cemetery (or because the body has already been interred), services can be scheduled in late afternoon or evening, which gives attendees a chance to take off from work a little early in order to attend or go after work.
- A memorial service, particularly coupled with cremation, is viewed by some as a cost-saver. In reality, money is a factor in many ritual choices, particularly when there has been tension in families or when financial resources to cover funeral expenses are limited.

Wolfelt dismisses such considerations, arguing that the memorial tends "to encourage mourners to skirt the healing pain that funerals" provide.

Alternative rituals

Increasingly, the ritual choice for some families is "D: none of the above" particularly when family members insist, "He wasn't very religious." Some prefer the "tribute" (so much that Alan Creedy thinks "tribute center" may become the new word for funeral home) or "the gathering" as an informal reception (2000, p. 34). But some would argue that viewpoint overlooks the reality that funerals are to support the living as well as to bury the dead. Thomas G. Long, former professor of homiletics at Princeton Seminary, after a year-long study of funeral rituals, comments: "If present trends continue, funeral directors and clergy can expect an increase in the pressure to become 'interior decorators of ritual,' designing environments, ad hoc services, and individualized occasions that suit this or that whim. In one sense, who cares . . . any clergy who perform weddings are quite experienced in meeting a myriad of idiosyncratic requests" (1997, October, p. 16).

Long concludes that those who are deprived of or deprive themselves of the great tradition of ritual resources in the religious community to create their own ritual "lite" "are dipping into a shallow well and will, in the long run, find themselves soon thirsty again" (p. 16). But it doesn't have to be all or nothing.

Nevertheless, the reality is that some friends want some innovative and creative experience that more likely reflects the personality of the deceased. Regardless, one funeral director concludes the role of rituals is to "give the community, friends, and family members the opportunity to show the deceased that one final act of love" (Pat Sefton, in McCormick, 2000, May, p. 22).

By offering clear leadership in ritual planning, ministers can partner with the funeral director and family to make sure that "final act of love" is an act Dissanayake calls "making special." She asks, for example, why one study of British motorcycle gangs revealed that when a member dies, the group turns to the established church for ritualization. It certainly was not because they were religious or accepted the church's teachings, "but because its ritual gave them a ready-made and widely recognized formal way to accord significance to the death" (Dissanayake, 1995, p. 138, citing Willis, 1978). That is true for others too.

Thus, pastors need not try to squeeze every family into a liturgical ritual mold. Rather, standardized liturgies are "resources and models of ritual wisdom that should inspire rather than constrain" (Anderson and Foley, 1997, p. 1003) something of a pattern. Maybe the wedding tradition of "Something old, something new, something borrowed, something blue" would be wise advice in planning funeral rituals also. Admittedly, some people come bearing memories of bad, awful, outrageous rituals. When they say, "I don't like funerals!" the minister may respond, "I've been to some I didn't like either. Tell me what it is that you don't like and let me see what I can do to come up with a ritual that will be appropriate."

Pastor-leaders hear out the idea rather than beginning with "Not in my church you won't!" In most cases, with some effort, there can be a win-win situation.

Innovation

My mother was a great handshaker. At the close of her funeral service, I asked the funeral director to remove the casket spray. Since in that community a final walk-by is traditionally required, I asked that each person, as a way of honoring Mother, would place a hand on the casket and leave a handprint. It was a very moving experience; obviously, there were different responses. But as we drove to the cemetery, the funeral director said to me, "I've seen a lot of things in my work, but that was incredible! Would you mind if I suggest that to other families?" Days later a pastor called, having heard about it. "Could I use this?" This little ritual innovation cost no money but had a meaningful effect on many who attended my mother's funeral.

The committal

The third element of ritualization is the committal of the body or disposition of cremated remains. For some, the committal is the most draining because of its finality. Historically, in the time before paid cemetery workers, the grave was opened and closed by family and friends. Among those who practice the Jewish faith, family members and friends fill in the grave, each putting in one shovel full of dirt as a powerful symbolic act (Magida, 1996), a tradition some are now using in non-Jewish committals.

But some Christians can be resourceful in explaining why they want to avoid the committal. For some, the cemetery is too final, too brutal, even with the artificial grass hiding the mound of dirt. In some regions, to maintain an efficient cemetery operation (and to avoid overtime charges, especially in cemeteries with unionized workers), mourners are actively discouraged from lingering in the cemetery.

Some families make the decision for others by selecting a private or family-only graveside service. However, some find the moments of lingering valuable, necessary for leave-taking as well as for socializing with other mourners. Phyllis Theroux described her experience after her friend Barbara Boggs Sigmund, mayor of Princeton, New Jersey, died: "A candlelight procession through silent Princeton followed the casket to its burial space. Then the family left, and five of Barbara's oldest friends remained behind. We surrounded the coffin as it descended, placed our hands upon its top, and reclaiming the hymn, 'Tantum Ergo' from our memories, we sang our old friend into the earth" (Theroux, 1990, October 21, p. C5).

This act on the part of the friends became a ritual within a ritual. Contemporary attitudes toward attending the committal are so at odds with the ancient tradition of the church. Todd Van Beck points out that from earliest times Christians have called graves "cemeteries," which means "sleeping places" (2000, p. 62). Commenting on the first three centuries of Christianity, considered "the Church of the Martyrs," Richard Rutherford found the "earliest witnesses to Christian care of the dead are the cemeteries themselves" (1980, p. 8). Christians ate a funeral meal in the cemetery and later celebrated the Eucharist among the tombs. So convinced were the early Christians that physical death did not terminate eternal life, "They had every hope that the life they once shared together in Eucharist would be theirs again in the eschatological kingdom" (p. 9). Over time, the graves of the martyrs became "places of special devotion" (p. 9) that invited pilgrimages. Eventually, churches were built on or near those graves.

Nevertheless, some desire to avoid the brutal reality of the grave at all costs. Some greeters will never go back to a cemetery, a reality that has fueled the concept of perpetual care sold by cemeteries. For some the reality of that last encounter is brutal.

I wrote about one individual's desire to avoid cemeteries in *Grieving the Death of a Friend:* "Now, my wife and I end it at the church or funeral home. I tell people that it's because, at my age, I don't drive so good any more. But that's just an excuse I've crafted. I drive better than most of my friends. But I just don't like those slow rides out to the cemetery especially on cold, wet, dreary days. It took me weeks last fall to get over burying my friend Herb. I got soaked in the cold rain but it was my heart that hurt the most, afterwards. But I do worry that when my time comes to ride in the hearse, no one will drive behind me on my last ride" (1996, p. 70).

Conclusion

Kenneth L. Woodward wrote that grief demands a rituals response because rituals contain healing powers that are "not solely of our own invention. To die alone is bad enough, but to grieve without rituals that lift the broken heart is worse. Those whose grief is affirmed within a wider community of faith are fortunate" (1997, September 22, p. 62).

Some people eventually complain of feeling cheated or deprived of a ritual, especially when they feel they were "talked out of it." These greeters may need an opportunity to create additional rituals, however long after the death, to recognize the significant losses of their lives. The Church has long recognized such a need through the observance of All Saints' Day (November 1 in Roman Catholic tradition) and All Souls' Day (November 2 among mainline Christians). In the Jewish tradition, such observance in marked through *Yizyor.*

When in doubt, have a ritual.
If necessary, create one!

Creating meaningful rituals

Kim Logan of Kansas City Hospice offers the following steps for creating meaningful rituals:
- Focus on a goal. What is the desired outcome?
- Plan. Let ideas flow, and pick and choose among them.

- Flesh out details before making a choice.
- Prepare. Gather the materials and resources that will be needed.
- Perform the ritual.
- Incorporate the ritual into the memory.
  I would add two more steps:
- Evaluate the ritual. Did it work? Did it not work? How might it be better improved for next time? Hopefully, as a pastoral care leader, you're keeping a journal to record observations and evaluations of the rituals you lead.
- Share with other clergy. Your discovery or innovation could be an enormous resource for other pastor-leaders.

Goal of Pastoral Leadership

My goal as a pastor-leader is to make funeral rituals more meaningful for all who experience them. These rituals so similar to others that I have led are to transition those who loved this particular individual from a world of presence to a world of memory. My goal is to make each ritual count.

A Spiritual Formation Exercise

1. Spend some moments recalling and reviewing the last funeral ritual you led or experienced.
2. Read Gen. 49:29—50:1-13, which tells about the death and burial of Jacob.
3. Pause. Ask God to speak to you through a fresh encounter with this scripture.
4. Now read the passage as you would a story to a child. Make the text come alive. At the end of the reading, write down six details you notice in this reading.

    1. _____   4. _____
    2. _____   5. _____
    3. _____   6. _____

5. Imagine yourself a participant in this funeral procession from Egypt to the cave in the field of Machpelah, near Mamre. Think of all the logistics involved in moving this very large company of mourners. It would have been much easier to bury Jacob in Egypt.
6. Read this part of verse 15: "When Joseph's brothers saw that their father was dead they said, 'What if Joseph holds a grudge against us?'" How did this fear influence their participation in the rituals?
7. Ask God to show you how this passage can be shared with greeters planning funerals and memorial services.

A Leadership Decision

As a result of reading this chapter, I need to remember to

1. _____

2. _____

A Story That Will Preach

Chicago sportscaster Harry Caray had a voice that could never be forgotten, especially his "Holy Cow!" uttered during a Chicago Cubs baseball game. He was, according to some, "bigger than life." Caray died in 1998. How do you ritualize such a public figure? At his funeral, priests cracked jokes and friends roasted the colorful baseball broadcaster for his "love and tireless commitment to the fans" (Breslin, 1998, p. 1). The outrageous, bigger-than-life dimensions of the deceased could not easily be portrayed or ignored in a traditional funeral mass in Holy Name Cathedral. Father Jerry Boland, president of the Catholic Archdiocesan Priests Council of Chicago, "explains" this approach to ritual:

> This is the direction we're moving in—to be more connected with people. That was what really struck people at Harry Caray's funeral. I think they thought some priest was going to get up there and talk about Jesus and the cross and never mention Harry. I would rather err on the side of personalizing too much than to err on the other side, where people go to a funeral and then say it could have been anybody *(cited in Breslin, 1998, p. 3)*.

And at the end of the mass, pallbearers slowly carried his casket up the long center aisle of the church to the tune of "Take Me Out to the Ballgame." Admittedly, Caray's widow, as chief mourner, had given participants great permission by saying, "Let it be a celebration."

Some pastor-leaders use a subtle approach in some funerals:

> It would be difficult to bury _____ without mentioning Jesus. The key decision in _____'s life was accepting Jesus as Lord and Savior. That decision turns this into a celebration not so much of _____'s life, but the life he [she] found in the resurrection of Jesus from the dead. We are not burying just anybody today—we are burying _____. In Jesus Christ he [she] became somebody!

When Jacob died, his sons took him back to that family plot in the field of Machpelah. It would have been impossible to miss so large a funeral procession. It was the lead feature on the local news that night. Obviously "the Canaanites who lived there" noticed just as non-Christians will notice this ritual. They said, "The Egyptians are holding a solemn ceremony of mourning" (Gen. 50:11). The ceremony was solemn because it reminded these mourners of who they were: children of Abraham and Sarah, Isaac and Rebekah, Jacob and Leah, and aliens in Egypt. Why go to so much bother with a ritual? Why make a big fuss? Because this ritual reminds us of who we are: we are children of the Heavenly Father—the Father who has now welcomed _____ home.

Rituals are a bridge between the world in which the loved one exists and an emerging world without the deceased.

11

Making Special

*Many Roman citizens would have characterized the
early Christian communities as burial societies!*
—Robert Wilken in Meador and Jones, 2000, August 16-23, p. 831

Key Point Summary

Ministry with the bereaving is about ministering with individuals. The pastor-leader welcomes the opportunity to lead decisively because this is the only funeral an individual is going to have for this loved one. The memory of this funeral and a pastor's leadership will last a lifetime.

Give permission to grieve

Many grievers need permission to grieve thoroughly and uniquely. For individuals in some faith communities, the pastor still is an authority and has influence to shape grief expression. Permission can be given both publicly and privately, but especially during the visitation and during the funeral or memorial service.

A Commitment
**As a pastor I will work to make this community of faith
a safe place to do the normal work of grief.**

Giving permission is a courageous act. Some of the most pious Christians in North America, and not a few secularists, have embraced this culture's mandate: *get over it as quickly as possible.*

Ask, "Who is being overlooked?" Then
- Call the griever.
- Send a note to the griever.
- Visit the griever.
- Share a resource or cassette with the griever.
- Pray for the griever.

Give yourself permission to grieve

Many pastors take on a distanced stance: Don't let them see *you* grieve. Why not? The writer of Acts reports, with no hint of apology, "Godly men buried Stephen and mourned deeply for him" (Acts 8:2). Jesus made no effort to hide His "deeply moved" and troubled spirit from the Jews after the death of Lazarus. In fact, His grief triggered cynics to say, "Could not he who opened the eyes of the blind man have kept him from dying?" (John 11:37). George Barna speaks to the barrier to transparency: "In the typical church, it is impossible for the pastor to be truly transparent about the struggles he endures with people within the church, within his family or within the ministry overall. So who pastors the pastor? Few churches have people skilled at doing so or who have a mind to do so. In essence, the pastor is on his own from the time he leaves seminary" (1993, p. 145).

What is the pastor to do? A pastor in Louisiana said, "When I know a particular funeral is going to be tough, I either ask a staff member or often a retired person in my congregation to attend as a designated prayer—especially to pray for me."

Obviously, the Scriptures contain numerous examples of grief. Ezekiel *"sat* among" the grievers for seven days "overwhelmed" (Ezek. 3:15). More challenging to ignore is Jesus' open display of grief at the tomb of Lazarus. What more eloquent expression of permission can there be than "Jesus wept" (John 11:35)? In those two words, pastor-leaders find permission to be human. As we once sang in Sunday School, "He the great example is a pattern for me." Although the culture says to "be professional," "ungrief" can lead only to isolation and alienation. Barna comments on the consequences of alienation: "Consequently, most pastors tell us they feel lonely in ministry. While they have many friends and acquaintances with whom they can share a good laugh and a pleasant evening, they have few people with whom they can share their hearts. The isolation they experience erodes some of the enthusiasm and the power they bring to ministry" (1993, p. 145).

The grief of a funeral often reactivates unprocessed grief from previous funerals. By rigidly controlling their public expression of grief, pastors miss teachable and reachable moments to model healthy grief to their parishioners, particularly males. The news that his brother Charles had died reached John Wesley too late for him to attend the funeral. Three weeks later, he was leading a service in Lancashire and was deeply moved by 100 boys and girls singing his brother's hymn "Come, O Thou Traveler Unknown." As was custom in that day, John "lined out" the first verse but was ambushed by the words, "My company before is gone, / And I am left alone with thee." Historian John Pollock describes the scene: "His voice faltered. He burst into tears, sat down in the pulpit, and covered his face with his hands. The congregation wept with him, and instead of song, the building was rent by cries. Then he recovered himself and preached and prayed, conducting a service which none would forget" (1989, pp. 246-47).

Give the congregation permission to grieve

The pastor-leader encourages the congregation to express its collective grief. The pastor-leader gives grievers permission to remember. Suppose I say: from now to the end of this chapter do not think of a hot fudge sundae. Put it right out of your mind. Do not think about the hot fudge cascading over the vanilla ice cream. Some readers are ready to head for Dairy Queen. Why? Because I

> **Memories allow me to care for my heart.**
> —Alan Wolfelt, 1997, p. 57

told you *not* to think of a hot fudge sundae. The same is true with memories. Pastors hamstring conversation by assuming a memory or a name to be an emotional land mine. Hardly. Consistently, grievers say that the failure to remember or mention the loved one's name wounds more.

Pastor-leaders use memories: "I still remember the time, Ryan. . . ." It's not coincidental at all that Jesus prefaced the Last Supper with these words: "Do this in remembrance of me" (1 Cor. 11:24). On how many Civil War monuments are the words "Lest we forget"? One of the themes flowing through Scripture is *remember.*

Observe colleagues

In making the commitment to do this book, I decided to attend as an observer at least 50 funerals or memorial services of individuals I did not know. I wanted to see clergy conduct funerals, particularly tough ones. My friend Don Lada, a funeral director in Michigan, often notices ministers attending funerals being conducted by peers. Why? Pastors can learn new skills and sensitivities. One of my favorite quotes came from a priest who led the funeral for a monk I did not know:

May all the tasks of today be opportunities for holiness.
—Abbot Barnabas, 2000, August 2, Benedictine Abbey, Atcheson, Kansas

The tasks of today—including leading a funeral or observing at a memorial service—may be enhanced because I obtained creative ideas from observing colleagues. I particularly recommend this practice for newly licensed and ordained ministers. One skill or idea could be an incredible resource for the pastor's equivalent of a "rainy day."

Befriend a funeral director

Talk about individuals who have seen and heard it all—funeral directors certainly fit that category. Pastor-leaders would do well to tap into their wisdom. Meet a funeral director for breakfast or coffee (easier on the schedule for both than lunch). After conducting a service with this director, ask for feedback, and ask for a recommendation of a pastor in the community to observe.

Even the best funeral directors have tough days and face soul-draining funerals and difficult-to-serve families. Relationships between director and family or director and pastor often unfold in stressed conditions, even by spiritual individuals. Identify any criticism of a funeral director or facility: what is direct observation, what is physically exhausted speculation, what is assumption? Remember not all funeral directors consider other funeral directors as colleagues; some choose to see them as competitors, despite advice from the leading mortuary consultant (Wolfelt, 2000, October) that such an attitude harms the entire profession.

Effective Pastor-Leaders

- Pay a courtesy call on funeral directors soon after arriving in a new community
- Take note of personnel changes at a funeral home
- Remember the funeral director's birthday or wedding anniversary
- drop notes of appreciation to funeral directors
- Build a bridge into their lives, professionally and personally
- Weigh any criticism of a particular funeral home or a funeral director

---

Get to know funeral directors in your community, because at the worse time in your life or the lives of your parishioners, you will want to deal with a friend and not a stranger.
—adapted from Barbara LesStrange, 2000, October, p. 46

Honor funeral directors in your community

Many churches have special recognition Sundays for schoolteachers, police, public servants, and so on. But rarely do congregations honor funeral directors, who are also servants of the community. Take a moment and think about Don Lada in Michigan, directing services for a six-year-old girl shot and killed by a classmate who brought a gun to school. Three round-the-clock days of dealing with a distraught family, an outraged community, and aggressive reporters from around the world were a continuous pressure cooker for this dedicated public servant. Who prayed for Lada? What would have happened during that traumatic experience if a minister had gone to him and said, "May I take a moment to pray for you?" or called and said, "Mr. Lada, I just wanted you to know that I'm praying for you today."

The negative attitude of some pastors toward funeral directors, that is, seeing them as adversaries taking advantage of people in a vulnerable moment, prevents healthy collegiality. Prayer is a way to build bridges.

No doubt you've said to a funeral director, "I don't know how you do it day in, day out." Although many funeral directors are committed Christians, the work schedule, or perhaps I should say the unpredictability of their work schedule, limits their involvement in their own churches. Many can be active only when they've become managers or owners (sometimes not even then). When the death call comes, the funeral director goes. Forget a child's birthday, the candlelight dinner with a spouse, the church board meeting—duty calls. Someone needs them *now*. But funeral directors need a pastor actively present in their lives.

Make no mistake: funeral directors are public servants just as much as police officers and fire personnel.

Funeral servanthood traces back to Nicodemeus and Joseph of Arimathaea, taking stewardship of Jesus' body despite heavy hearts, and to those courageous women moving in the darkness toward the tomb with spices to anoint the body of Jesus (Russell, 1996, October). (In the haste to bury Jesus before sundown and the start of the Jewish Sabbath, the preparations had been suspended.)

Encourage will-making and updating

Nothing can be more chaotic than to die intestate, either without a will or without an up-to-date will. When people tell me that they are pro-family, I respond, "Show me your will."

A will is critical when there are children or stepchildren who are minors; for individuals who have had multiple marriages, own a family business, or have significant assets. An individual can be worth more dead than alive in a wrongful death or accident.

I know a pastor who brings up the issue of a will in every funeral sermon. Why? "As a pastor," he explains, "I have seen too many surprises that leave widows and children in dire economic positions." Even Abraham had to interrupt his grief to haggle with the owner of the land on which he wanted to bury Sarah (Gen. 23:1-20).

Be prepared

The pastor-leader has a funeral text and sermon-in-the-works for the unexpected funeral. This file contains notes, possible texts, and ideas. Pastor Jim Henry disclosed that two weeks before Payne Stewart's funeral, he had felt inspired to prepare three sermons that week, something he had never done in 40 years as a busy pastor. "I thought, 'Lord, you have given me this to get ahead—time that I will need soon" (Guest, 2000, p. 47). Thus, the day before the service was a time to polish the sermon rather than frantically prepare.

Keep Memorial Day

The fourth commandment says, "Remember the Sabbath day, to keep it holy" (Exod. 20:8, KJV). If only there were a similar commandment for Memorial Day (in the United States) or Remembrance Day (in Canada). Some readers remember when these holidays were a time purely devoted to honoring the dead, particularly veterans. In the United States, the observance of Memorial Day was influenced by the fact that many churches, particularly in rural communities, owned cemeteries. A workday was needed before summer started. Tidying up the cemetery became a community event mixing maintenance work with social interaction and meals. I fear that when the World War II veterans die off, traditional Memorial Day will end. The change was accelerated when the United States Congress turned Memorial Day into a long weekend.

Memorial Day to many in the United States is little more than the first weekend of summer. It's a day for a trip to the beach, the lake, the ballpark, or a day for a backyard barbecue.

Unfortunately, many cemetery ceremonies are primarily secular or patriotic with only a token prayer by a minister. However, the Sunday of Memorial Day or Remembrance Day is your opportunity. Pastor-leaders creatively and deliberately use a hymn such as "For All the Saints" or the song "Find Us Faithful."

Follow the Wesleys and honor All Saints' Day (November 1). In the 10th century, at the urging of Odilio of Cluny, the church added "All Souls' Day." Liturgical churches traditionally recognize the "capital S" saints on November 1. Lynn C. Ramshaw asks, "But what about all those wonderful ones never canonized, officially recognized, by anyone? Who have died and still mean life to us?" (Williams, 2000, October, p. 7). These "faithful departed" make up some of what John the Revelator called "a great multitude that no one could count, from every nation, tribe, people and language, standing before the throne and in front of the Lamb" (Rev. 7:9). John reports that an elder asks, "Who are they, and where did they come from?" (v. 13). I could answer, "They include our loved ones who have come from small churches and megachurches, from rural churches to suburban churches. They were faithful followers of Jesus."

Use the Sunday of Memorial Day or Remembrance Day, or the Sunday before All Souls' Day, to preach on death and resurrection hope (a theme that should not be limited to Easter). That's why Christians sing, "Wonderful story of love! / Tell it to me again." And again. Ask your congregation to submit the names of those "faithful departed" they wish remembered. In the service, take time to call the roll (make sure you know how to pronounce the names).

One of the strong memories I have as a boy attending Nazarene district assemblies was the memoirs service, called "a special order of the day." At that point the business, sometimes the debate, of an assembly, was suspended so that those of the district who had died during the past year could be named. On many districts, this has now been abbreviated to a list of names on a sheet in the delegates' packet. This silent efficiency communicates, "We have more important business." In reality, it will not matter until your loved one is on the list. We need on a local church, district, and general church level a way creatively to "name" our dead.

Admittedly, leaders have to develop such an emphasis in increments. And leaders can expect some resistance or criticism, sometimes from certain grievers. Use open altar time as a time to pray for grievers in the church family. Invite them to gather at the altar. Take time to lay your hand on the head of each one and pray specifically for him or her. Anoint grievers.

Name those whom members of the congregation have lost in the last 12 months. Call the names aloud. Ask the congregation to respond responsively with this Spanish exclamation after each name is called: *Presente!* (Present!) Some will fondly remember roll call from school. This signifies *the* roll call. The choir might offer a stirring rendition of "When the roll is called up yonder."

Naming is not something new. For centuries, the roll call of saints who had joined the Church Triumphant was a regular part of worship, especially Communion. We, on the other hand, list the names of the donors and their loved ones who contribute Easter lilies or Christmas poinsettias and place plaques around a church to honor memorial gifts. But eventually humans forget. Why? Because we don't say the name aloud.

We need to find other ways to remind congregations to remember those who faithfully followed the Lord. A church web page may be one appropriate contemporary response.

It's also important to pause on other special days to remember that some grievers will find red-letter Sundays (Fathers' Day, Mothers' Day, Valentine's Day) bittersweet. I have never forgotten a Mothers' Day service in 1979 in which Paul Cunningham, then pastor of College Church of the Nazarene in Olathe, Kansas, spoke to the congregation before the service began. He welcomed visitors present for Mothers' Day and commented on the corsages and the plans for special brunches. Then he paused. "But we must not forget that for some here today, this is a bitter-sweet day. Loss clouds the day. Maybe you've lost your wife or your mother—and all the emphasis on Mother's Day is tearing you apart. Don't miss out on the chance to be part of *this* service. Let God get close to you this morning." What sensitivity!

Years later, in that same church, Dennis Apple organized a "Mothers' Day: Day to Remember" service in the afternoon for those in the church and in the community who had lost their mothers. What a compassionate means to redeem the day for many who had lost their mothers! Each participant was presented a colored ribbon on which the mother's name was written in calligraphy. At a certain point, each mother's name was called, and a son or daughter was invited to come forward and tie that ribbon on a large grapevine wreath. Then the person stepped to the microphone and shared one characteristic of his or her mother that he or she would never forget. It was a "time out" in a day of celebration to honor the bereaving. By the end of the service the stark brownness of the wreath had given way to a beautiful symbol of memory and love.

I have long wanted to rewrite the lyrics we sing, "When one has a heartache we all shed a tear" by inserting the word *initially.* I recall one Christmas worshiping with friends at Nashville First Church of the Nazarene. After a stirring singing of "Joy to the World," Pastor Millard Reed led into pastoral prayer time: "Oh, I'm so excited. Are you? I've been to so many Sunday School class parties. And all of my surprises are *still* surprises. But as pastor, I'm aware that in the midst of all the celebration and joy, there are people hurting all across this congregation. And if you're hurting from a death or illness or divorce or whatever, I don't want you to miss out on this time of prayer. So this morning, would you, in your pain, join me around this altar?"

And many did. Twenty-five years later, recalling this example of decisive pastoral leadership made tears fill my eyes. That Sunday morning many—including me—found a little package called hope. Why? Because a caring pastor took time to reach out to those he knew were in pain. That Sunday morning a caring pastor gave permission to grieve in the midst of a joyous service in a holiday season.

Build resources

Pastor-leaders gather resources for both a personal library and for the church library. Many grievers read. Some grievers tell me, "I read everything I can get my hands on." Professionals call this "bibliotherapy."

The pastor-leader is aware that New Age philosophy runs like a soft brook through grief literature. Several best-sellers in the grief section of your local bookstore or library are either unapologetically or thinly disguised New Age philosophy. A pastor can't read everything. So he or she enlists sensitive members to read for him. The pastor-leader is prepared when a grieving parishioner asks, "What do you think about this book?"

The pastor-leader initiates the conversation by asking, "What are you reading?" By having a list of spiritually healthy grief reading to recommend, good shepherds offer solid selections.

Initially, some grievers can't read. So I have developed "refrigerator quotes." Key quotes, no more than a paragraph, are blown up in large font, one per page. I ask grievers to put these encouraging quotes on their refrigerators as reminders for themselves and as encouragement for others who may see them. Ask grievers in your congregation to supply you brief quotations that have helped them.

Someone in your church might be able to take these quotations and dress them up with computer graphics. Periodically, a quotation can be dropped in the mail to grievers as "griefgrams," particularly on anniversaries of the death: one week, one month, six months, one year, and so on.

Grievers "pass on" grief books. Ask them to consider donating good books on grief to the church library. Set up memorial donations to your church library to honor loved ones. What a wonderful way to continue their memory through purchasing books to have available to loan or give away! It's wonderful to recommend a book, but some grievers will never get around to locating the book or buying it, let alone reading it. Give them a copy with perhaps a section highlighted or marked with a piece of ribbon. In this age of video, many libraries include resources from Wintergreen.

> More than 9 out of 10 senior pastors have read Christian books in the past year. On average, they read about 10 Christian books each year. In addition, two-thirds read about 4 non-Christian books in search of help annually.
> —George Barna, 1993, p. 144

Paul requested, "Bring . . . my scrolls, especially the parchments" (2 Tim. 4:13) as a way of staying prepared. The injunction to "Preach the Word; be prepared in season and out of season" (1 Tim. 4:2) means that pastor-leaders anticipate deaths and include this topic in their reading.

Anticipatory reading on grief can prepare you to be of help. I would also recommend that pastor-leaders have on hand for reference one of the standard grief texts such as Corr, Nabe, and Corr's *Death & Dying, Life & Living* or DeSpelder and Strickland's *The Last Dance: Encountering Death and Dying.*

Audit

In an era when success is the prima facie criterion for evaluating a pastor's success in ministry, important things, such as being with the bereaved, falls by the wayside as too time-consuming. One pastor told me, "If I followed your advice, I'd spend all my time in funeral homes and with grieving people. I'd never get anything done!" These days, some pastors are deciding and clearly communicating: "I do not have time to spend with the bereaving."

Pastors examine their effectiveness and the effectiveness of their congregations in every area except funerals. How can you "audit" your performance?

- What would happen if grieving families routinely were sent forms on which to evaluate clergy performance?
- What would happen if completed evaluations were not only seen by the pastor but reviewed by ecclesiastical authorities?
- What if part of pastoral care was an honest confrontation with the questions "How did I do?" and "Where was I insensitive?"
- What if sometime after the ritual, there was an honest dialogue with the family or friends on your involvement in the rituals? Might another family not benefit from such a performance review?

The importance of this funeral

This funeral could be someone's moment to meet God, to forgive a wound, to offer up a wound for healing. The pastor-leader knows that amazing things happen in the presence of a corpse.

Goal of Pastoral Leadership

Ministry with the bereaved is about leading individuals and "this time only" congregations. The pastor-leader recognizes the opportunity to "do good" to those who make up a household of grief. The memory of the pastor's leadership will last a lifetime. Thus, pastors seek to be welcome guests in the family's grief journey. Pastor-leaders take every funeral seriously—even those for strangers.

Spiritual Formation Moment

1. Read the following verse fragments from Solomon's petition for wisdom: "I am only a little child and do not know how to carry out my duties. . . . So give your servant a discerning heart to govern your people and to distinguish between right and wrong. For who is able to govern this great people of yours?" (1 Kings 3:7, 9).
2. Insert the word *lead* for *govern* in this passage. Is it easy for you to make this confession?
3. Speak to God about your thoughts and emotions in light of the contents of this chapter.

4. Ask God to give you understanding on how to lead grievers in your care.
5. Sing these words from "Rescue the Perishing":
   > *Down in the human heart, Crushed by the tempter,*
   > *Feelings like buried that grace can restore.*
   > *Touched by a loving heart, Wakened by kindness,*
   > *Chords that are broken will vibrate once more.*
   > *Rescue the perishing. Care for the [bereaving].*
   > *Jesus is merciful; Jesus will save.*
   >
   > —Fanny J. Crosby
6. Take a moment and audit your "perishing" list. Speak to God about each one.

A Story That Will Preach

In World War I, the German Navy disrupted British shipping lanes. War supplies were torpedoed to the bottom of the North Sea until British prime minister Lloyd George ordered that the cargo ships have escorts and travel in a protected group. The convoys reduced losses to just 1.1 percent of trade (Island, 1998, p. 19) and changed naval warfare.

Lofland (1982) argues that children need a "convoy of friends" to help them navigate childhood. Oltjenbruns (1995) insists that children require a convoy of support to survive the death of a childhood playmate. Adults and adolescents also need a convoy of "you can count on me" friends during this experience called grief. Even when the network of friends is small or scattered geographically, grievers need an "I'll be there for you" convoy of friends.

Grievers need supporters to help them navigate through the mine-fields of life, especially bereavement.

According to Kahn and Antonucci, an individual's convoy "consists of the set of persons on whom he or she relies for support and those who rely on him or her for support" (1980, p. 269).

A Leadership Decision

As a result of reading this chapter

1. _____
2. _____

Lord, give me a leading heart that I may walk faithfully alongside those trying to make sense of grief. Remind me that I have been called by You to be Your ambassador in this unfamiliar landscape called bereavement. In Jesus' name I pray. Amen.

12

Empowering a Congregation for Ministry with the Grieving

Leaders are measured by the extent to which they help develop those under their direction.
—Lawrence Appley, 1974, p. 88

⌒

Key Point Summary

Individuals experiencing loss are particularly receptive to care and sensitive to insensitivity on the part of the pastor or congregation. By empowering a congregation to invest in this critical arena of servanthood, the pastor leader sensitizes, equips, and resources laypeople to develop and use care skills.

By this point in the book, some pastors are asking, "How can I even begin to meet the demands on me?" Hunter (2000) answers, "In the most effective churches . . . lay people do most of the very regular hospital visitation, much of the counseling, most of the pastoral care, most of the visitation of unchurched people, and most of the visible community involvement" (p. 85). Then what does the pastor do? Hunter asserts that the pastor serves as "a 'manager' who is employed to get things done through other people" (p. 85).

A pastor-leader and a congregation must ask, How can I/we help this individual grieve thoroughly? How can this congregation support this griever? After the rituals, a pastor and congregation must evaluate their responses.

Clergy cannot do all of the grief care in a congregation. In Judaism, members of the synagogue's *chevra kadisha,* or "holy society," are responsible for the care and ritual washing of the corpse. These individuals are "on call," because most Jews will be buried before sundown of the next day. Each local church needs an appropriate "holy society" composed of lay volunteers who have been trained to make a difference when death touches a congregation.

**Six words summarize pastoral care with the bereaving:
"Somebody say something! Somebody do something!"
More accurately it's "Somebody *be* something!"**

Christians have long been involved in preparing the dead for burial. According to the writer of Acts, after the death of Dorcas, "her body was washed and placed in an upstairs room" (9:37) apparently by the same widows who later eulogized her charitable works to Peter. Although she was raised from the dead after Peter prayed, the service of the widows is my point. Many of the roles that Christians once faithfully performed, such as laying-out, washing, shroud-weaving, quilt-making (initially used for wrapping the body before caskets were commonly used, then for lining caskets), have been assumed by individuals who "undertook" to prepare the dead for burial. Within five decades from when the undertaker began functioning as a funeral director, many traditional acts of compassion had been transferred into the mortician's roster of duties, particularly in urban areas (White, 1994). This professionalization of compassionate care has been costly. Hali Weiss states that we have made ourselves more powerless in hiring professionals to handle death for us. "The result is a widening gap between our experience of death and the culture's treatment of it; over time this makes loss more difficult to bear" (1997, September 10, p. A11).

Performing these tasks for others was an apprenticeship for one's own eventual losses. By shared caring, individuals had some idea of what to expect. Fortunately, Weiss points to a growing movement seeking to reclaim death care from the professionals. For example, among Mexican immigrants, males may want to dig the grave as a way to be helpful but also as a way to save the family the cost of opening the grave (Crespo, 1996, September). (Some cemeteries prohibit this because of liability issues.) Some individuals are asking for the right to "close" the grave rather than have cemetery employees do so with a backhoe (which, although efficient, seems less caring).

The role of women

Historically, compassionate care was "almost always performed and presided over by women" (White, 1994, p. 79). Grief care skills were passed on from grandmother or mother to daughter. Certainly the heavier tasks of moving, bearing, and actually burying the body—especially after the development of the casket, which significantly increased the lifting demands on bearers—were performed by males. Males moved furniture—no doubt under the supervision of women—so that the body could be viewed in the parlor of the home. In many communities males gathered to build a casket; others dug the grave or carved a headstone. These physical tasks gave males ways to "do" their grief and to reminisce.

Christians—particularly women from the 5th, 10th, or 15th centuries—would be dumbstruck to hear contemporary believers say, "I just wish there were something (or something *more*) I could do." Until recent times (and still in many areas of the world) if the necessary things got done, they were done by neighbors and friends. The church, the hub of the community, provided manpower. People attended churches in their immediate neighborhood. (The development of automobiles and interstates created the arena of the megachurch.)

Grievers purchase these services today. Thus, when someone says to the family, "Is there anything I can do?" generally a family member can accurately respond, "No, I think everything's taken care of." Yet, ironically we complain about the high cost of funerals.

An Old Testament model of serving

People want to be helpful. How can pastor-leaders equip laity? A look at Jeremiah's experience of receiving servant hospitality provides valuable insights. What would have happened had Ebed-Melech not intervened? With the king's permission, Ebed-Melech recruited 30 men to lift Jeremiah from the cistern (Jer. 38:10). Apparently some pulled, some protected while the sensitive eunuch supervised. (The eunuch may have been physically unable to pull Jeremiah out—but he could manage the compassion. In some congregations today, individuals who are homebound have been enlisted into the important ministry of praying for and keeping in contact with the grieving.)

Ebed-Melech, in a rare display of sensitivity in crisis, padded the ropes before pulling. What a significant symbolic example for congregational care!

It is one thing to care but something else to express care in a way that does not further complicate the grief.

Ways a congregation can pad the ropes

A congregation can "pad the ropes" by empowering members to see and seize the opportunity sensitively to "do good to all people, especially those who belong to the family of believers" (Gal. 6:10)—not just to do minimal "good," but to offer "generous hospitality" (Scott, 2000, p. 116). Shelley (2000) comments, "With individualism and isolation increasing, the need for community is stronger than ever" (p. 34). The church has a way of extending good to those who make up a "temporary" community.

1. Decide to be available to offer help

A congregation needs to do a needs assessment for responding to particular grievers. A response could be different if there's a large number of family and guests coming from out of town than if most of the family live in the community. In a rural community, the needs may not be those of an urban area where drive time must be taken into consideration in decision-making, planning rituals, and compassion care. In a rapidly transitioning community (that is, rural to suburban), a growing church may ask, "Who are we now, now that we're no longer a small church in a rural area?" On the other hand, a church that has experienced significant decline must ask, "How do we offer compassionate care *now?*"

> **The focus for any congregation's grief care is**
> **wrapped up in three questions:**
> **What shall we do?**
> **What shall we *not* do?**
> **What shall we do well?**

Blair (1998) counsels church leaders, "You can do yourself and your church [as well as the families who will be the recipients of your help] an important service by setting some systems in place to be ready when they are needed" (p. 37) so that valuable time is not lost organizing a response. In large churches, it will be wise to have multiple teams that can be activated within moments of notification of death. Each team will have apprenticeships learning particular skills in grief care.

> **Every congregation needs a standing grief**
> **care task force to respond like a volunteer**
> **fire department summoned by an alarm.**

Sometimes, particularly after a long illness, a house needs to be cleaned, particularly if out-of-town guests will be staying there or meal functions will be held there. Members of a team respond to the "smallest of tasks," such as cleaning the house, scrubbing toilets, running loads of laundry, and vacuuming as well as focused tasks such as answering the door and telephone, running errands, notifying and coordinating and recording food donations, preparing food, planning and delivering hospitality. One church, for example, keeps "a compassion closet" well stocked with plastic and paper goods so that team members do not have to ask grievers, "Where do you keep your paper towels [and so on]?"

Given the number of homes burglarized during funerals, providing individuals to be in the residence during the rituals is helpful. Moreover, in the family's absence, this can be an ideal time to clean.

Congregations are empowered to be effective when members make themselves available.

2. Jettison the clichés

Members of a congregation can serve up clichés to grievers faster than burgers in fast-food establishments. Grievers commonly endure statements like

"It's all for the best."
"She's [He's] in a better place."
"God must have a reason."
"We all have to go sometime."
"Life goes on!"
"He [She] lived a good, long life."
"She's [He's] not suffering anymore."
"You have to be strong."
"God never puts more on us than we can bear."

In times of grief, too many Christians have this modus operandi: "Don't just stand there—say something!" Clichés are verbal shorthand. Why struggle for words when a cliché will do? Unfortunately, clichés take on a life of their own and remain in emotional perpetual motion, ricocheting through the canyons and hearts of the bereaving. A fresh round of wounding can take place whenever grievers recall the cliché. Donald Howard (1979, 1998), an Australian pastor and widower, bemoans the "assault of clichés" from "well-meaning people who were clumsy in their approach" (p. 14).

Clichés can bruise the soul as effectively as a baseball can bruise the skin.

Even Scripture verses used as clichés compound grief. Anne Donovan describes her reaction following the death of her stillborn baby when well-meaning friends sent a poem that suggested, "God looked around heaven and decided that it needed some brightening up, so he plucked a vivid flower" (that is, Anne's unborn baby). Anne adds, "I just clenched my teeth to keep from saying something I'd regret" (Donovan, 1998, September 19, p. 8).

Unfortunately, people who use clichés in such times go unchallenged. Congregations are empowered to be effective when members are sensitized to clichés and easy answers.

3. Say the name

Amazingly, the well-meaning begin "pronoun-ing," using "he" or "she" rather than the deceased's actual name soon after the death. Even grievers begin using relationship words instead of the name: "my husband," "my wife," "my mother," "my son."

An individual is not "gone" until two things happen: you stop saying his or her name and you stop telling stories about him or her.

In too many congregations, the name of a deceased person will never be mentioned again after the funeral; in others, never after the first Sunday following the funeral, except perhaps in a prayer request. Admittedly, the name may be printed in a worship folder for a poinsettia at Christmas or a lily at Easter, but rarely will the name be spoken. Many erroneously assume saying the name, in a worship setting or in conversation with a griever, will be painful for the family.

Even families in grief and friends collude to avoid saying the name. "Whatever you do, do not say X's name" because "it might upset X" or "She might start crying." Avoiding saying the name makes conversations awkward and suggests, "If these people forgot him, they'll forget *me* after *I'm* dead." A pastor-leader models saying the name so that members of the congregation will follow that lead. Congregations are empowered to be effective when members understand they don't have to avoid saying the name.

> People think it hurts me to hear my wife's name. It doesn't. I think "Barbara" is the most beautiful name in the world. But I see people skid to a halt having almost said the name. That's what hurts me the most: when they almost said *Barbara.* Go ahead and say her name.
> —Ben, a widower

4. Volunteer presence and assistance

Members of a congregation effectively serve when they fulfill promises made to the grieving. The angriest participant I have ever had in a Grief Gathering demanded, "I want to know—where are the people who made all the promises at the funeral home? Where are the ones who promised, 'Oh, now, you just call us if there's anything you need.' Where are they when I need them?"

Promises punctuate the clichés at visitations and funerals. Some people make promises never expecting the "coupons to be clipped," as my friend Harry Dickerson liked to say.

Too often promises may be just another cliché or something to say when you don't know what to say.

One widow explains, "It's not that they say 'no' if you ask for assistance. They hesitate: 'Uh, let me check with my husband [wife].' What's to check?" Another widow adds, "They stall—'Uh, let me get back to you,' but they never do." One widower defends the promise-breakers, "It's not that people don't intend to keep promises—it's just that everyone's so busy these days."

Rather than asking, "Is there anything I can help you do?" or "Call me if there's anything I can do for you," people should make specific suggestions: "May I help you . . . [clean out closets, address thank-you notes, and so on]?" By suggesting specific tasks, the person lifts the weight of requesting from the grieving to himself or herself. Congregations are empowered to be effective when members make only the promises they intend to keep.

5. Attend funeral rituals

Attending a ritual, particularly the funeral, is one way members can support through presence, even when they don't know the deceased well or at all, say in the case of the funeral for a friend's father.

Attendance is more than being polite or social. It can be a ministry of presence.

Historically, Christians have postponed burial so that friends might "come and weep and take their last look" (Basilios, 1991, p. 425) and extend condolences to family and other members of "the household of faith" (Gal. 6:10, KJV). The visitation also gives the Christian community the chance to witness the promises of future assistance. Little wonder Luke wrote this of the Early Church: "There were no needy persons among them" (Acts 4:34). Why? Believers showed up, made promises, and then kept their promises. Our casual attitude toward a visitation would have been outrageous to previous generations of believers. During my apprenticeship as a funeral director, I watched families without a large social network or who were nominal members of a congregation sit alone in a parlor. But I watched them light up when, although strangers, persons walked in and announced, "We're from the church."

Does your congregation have a designated driver to assist senior adult members who would like to attend the visitation or funeral but don't drive? Are your members likely to ask, "Wonder if _____ would like to go with us to the visitation or funeral?"

Those who attend a funeral, Gerkin (1997) reminds, make up "a community of memory" (p. 122) and worship. Ken Hemphill (1999) opened a funeral for an individual killed in the shootings at Wedgwood Baptist Church in Fort Worth, Texas,

> **We need the presence of others, we need the presence of God, to stand with us in our grief.**
> **—James Wall, 1997, p. 819**

with this invocation: "We worship you [God] in our grief" (Jones, 1999, p. 11A). Through active rather than passive participation in funeral worship, God's people are reminded of "who they are" (Gerkin, 1997, p. 123), and nonbelievers are introduced to who they could become. Never have I heard anyone call a funeral in a mortuary chapel "a worship experience."

By attending the funeral, members also support the pastor as he or she participates in the ritual. "Believe me," one pastor noted. "It helps me get through the tough funerals if I can look out and see a familiar face."

Attending a funeral ritual is an act of Christian hospitality— a servant act shaped by a willingness to be inconvenienced and to be touched by the grief of another individual.

Another advantage is that by attending, members have opportunity to experience a good funeral and are more likely to make better decisions when they themselves plan funeral rituals.

6. Cooking

In the Greek Orthodox Christian tradition, funeral meals are called "mercy meals," which reflects the reality that for generations, when people have not known what to say or do, they head to the kitchen. Although grieving people may not feel like eating, it's essential that they maintain their strength for the demanding work of active grief. The availability of food facilitates hospitality and conversation in the immediate funeral period, particularly when guests, perhaps from out of town, visit the primary residence.

Good food around a familiar table can become a type of communion.

Preparing food for the family is increasingly becoming a thing of the past, or more common in "traditional communities," although Pokorski (1995) laments that there "aren't as many traditional communities around as there used to be" (p. 68). Preparing a casserole, salad, or dessert is a "concrete and helpful" response (Searl, 1993, p. 111) that promotes a sense of usefulness. Some find that baking or cooking re-boots a pleasant memory.

Preparing food traces back to the Jewish custom of sitting *shiva.* Jewish grievers could not leave their homes for one week following the death of a family member. In the days before refrigerators, freezers, instant foods, and microwave ovens, let alone fast food, the faith community fed the family for that week (Brener, 1993). Moreover, this tradition not only prevented mourners from isolating themselves but also gave people practical ways to help through preparing the *seudas havrah,* meals of grief.

Christians zealously adapted the practice. The outpouring of food has overwhelmed more than one griever— "Look at all this food!" Food preparation at a time of death has traditionally been considered "women's work" (White, 1994, p. 79). However, the recent movement of large numbers of women from homemaking into the workplace has impacted hospitality patterns, even in churches and rural communities. Increasingly in urban areas, churches prepare one benevolence meal rather than multiple meals. Fast-food establishments, delicatessens, and supermarkets are the caterers of convenience. Thus, a busy church friend can pick up a bucket or tray "of something" to take to the family and only be minimally inconvenienced—but, I would contend, only minimally blessed. Moreover,

> **When my friend Judy died I headed to the kitchen and started cooking—after all, Judy has three teenage boys who are hungry all the time. But I lost it while preparing the Mexican salad that I am known for. Judy had pestered me for the recipe for years, but even after I gave it to her, hers still didn't quite taste like mine. As I carried the salad over there, all I thought about was the many times our families had eaten together.**
>
> **—Marion, friend**

the disposable container means there is nothing to wash or return. However, this eliminates the important secondary ritual of returning a dish, bowl, pan or tray, days or weeks after the ritual, which facilitates an opportunity to initiate conversation: "How are you doing? Do you have time to talk or for a cup of coffee?"

When my mother died, the church prepared lunch for the family after the funeral. I noticed that the servers and preparers were retired adults from the church, some of whom had worshiped for decades with my mother; the experience must have been bittersweet.

Mention must be made of preparing grief meals for the nominal or inactive member or for those whom church growth leaders call "stakeholders" (Hunter, 2000, p. 62). Indeed, in many of the fast-growing churches, constituents are not identified as members per se. Moreover, since some people are part of several congregations, churches may need to coordinate hospitality.

The danger of perceived favoritism occurs when a well-known member (or a family member of a well-known or influential member) dies, and the hospitality response may be generous. But what is the response for the "hardly known" or "once known" member? All the more reason to have a committee to administer, supervise, and evaluate hospitality, giving attention to the Early Church's scandal over hospitality. Two essential characteristics for providing care were for the givers to be "full of the Spirit and wisdom" (Acts 6:3).

Congregations are empowered to be effective when pastors, staff, and members feed the bereaving.

7. Write notes and send cards

Many people are quick to say, "In situations like this, I'm just not good with words." That reality stimulates the creativity and profits of the greeting card companies. One of the early actions of individuals upon learning of a death is to buy (Morgan, 1994) and send a sympathy card. Many consider sending a card to be "the least I can do." Actually, it's important to select an appropriate card, given the circumstances of some deaths, particularly murder or suicide. Hallmark's slogan, "When you care enough to send the very best" underlies the importance of finding "just the right card" and not a generic, could-have-been-sent-to-any-griever card.

Selecting and sending a card can be a dual-comforting process: the recipient and the sender are both blessed.

Those who cannot attend the services can send cards. Members should be reminded that cards sent with only a signature might be perceived as less caring. Researchers find that older adults are more likely to add a handwritten note on a sympathy card to personalize it (Caldwell, McGee, and Pryor, 1998).

Increasingly, in a multicultural society, Christians will need to send cards to individuals who practice other world religions. In haste, some do not consider how the recipient will receive the card. Rabbi Earl Grollman comments that sympathy cards with a cross or a New Testament scripture may bring comfort to the sender but be considered insensitive by a member of another world religion. What to do?

Compassionate Christians should be cautious in selecting Scripture to add to a sympathy card. Certainly, all things will work together for the good of those who know and loved the Lord, but Rom. 8:28 can be a whack upside the heart of a grief-stricken Christian.

Caldwell, McGee, and Pryor (1998) echo Ann Landers's advice that instead of mailing a condolence card, when possible you should personally take it to the grievers. Members also need to send cards weeks, months after the death, particularly for hard "firsts" for grievers: Valentine's Day, Christmas, Mothers' Day, Fathers' Day. Grievers may be avalanched initially but treasure cards that come on an anniversary, a birthday, Valentine's Day—sometimes with only a simple handwritten message such as "Thinking of you today."

> Better still send an individual letter with your personal memories as a permanent record to be read in the days and weeks and years ahead.
> —Earl Grollman, 1993, p. 29

Congregations are empowered to be effective through sending caring cards and letters.

8. Again compassionate care

In too many congregations, there is a "window" of compassion care for approximately 30 days. Then the church, taking its signals from the culture, withdraws, thereby subtly suggesting "It's time to move on." In some congregations, another family has now moved to the "center ring" of compassion.

Many churches are more inclined to offer care during the initial period following the death and rituals when what-needs-to-be-done-now-or-next is reasonably clear. Some grievers may be too numb initially to appreciate a care touch. But down the road, they will.

When grievers verbalize or complain of the lack of attention or insensitivity, the first response is to be defensive: "We *sent* flowers and cards, we *prepared* meals, we *showed up* at the viewing . . . ," which sets up the unspoken question, "What *more* could he [she] expect?"

Using a hospital analogy, many churches offer excellent emergency room services or intensive care. Some churches (and some pastors) thrive on crisis. We're like the Red Cross: on the scene with resources immediately. The problem occurs when the patient needs long-term care or the equivalent of rehabilitation outpatient services. How can a congregation respond?

Call again	Visit again
Invite again	Listen again
Offer again	Pray again

Some would respond, "We offered to go by and bring her to the fellowship dinner, but she said no." The "no" may have been to a specific request on a specific day. Unfortunately, many Christians ask grievers once or twice and then stop asking. *Ask again.*

Congregations are empowered to be effective when members repeat their expressions of compassion.

9. Recognize anniversary grief

In a hurry-up culture, the noting of anniversaries of the death may appear to some to be pathological, a resistance to the desired goal of "moving on." Rather, honoring anniversaries is the healthy griever's way of acknowledging the long-term demands and dimensions of grief.

Our minds function like archivists storing all kinds of data for future reference or recall. Key dates count on the calendars of our souls.

Pastor-leaders (and the lay leaders they train) assist individuals in finding ways to honor the day and the memories. Still, many must remember clandestinely. In fact, after moving to a new congregation, it may be years before a pastor discovers the full grief narratives of some in the congregation. Computer records can help church staffs monitor death anniversaries. It takes only a moment for a member of the pastoral staff or a designated layperson to drop a note or to call to say, "I know today is important to you. I'm thinking of you and praying specifically for you."

Anniversaries can also be acknowledged and honored through sponsoring altar flowers on the Sunday nearest the anniversary and by acknowledging the gift not only in the worship folder but also verbally. Books, videotapes, or other resources could be donated to the church library or another ministry in honor of the deceased.

Pastor-leaders establish a "wish list" in varying amounts for needs of the church that can be addressed through an anniversary memorial gift.

11. Make sacred space safe for grievers

Grievers need safe spaces and safe places in which to do grief work, places where grievers need not apologize for emotions or for grief itself, where "still grieving" is not a confession of weakness. Some churches encourage brief grief by applauding those who are "getting on with their lives." The griever will be reminded that the deceased "is in a better place" and that "God knows best." Some grievers may not find that safety in their own families (or with particular family members or friends).

Pastor-leaders never assume that
family members are talking about the death.

After her husband's premature death and her experiences of denial by friends, Madeleine L'Engle (1996) cautioned, "We cannot grieve in any healthy way in total isolation—solitude, yes, but not isolation. Grief, like Christianity, is shared by the entire body. Nothing that affects one part of the body does not affect it all" (p. 253). Her assertion is captured in a popular chorus about heartache sung in many contemporary worship settings, that is, unfortunately, more easily sung than practiced in congregational life.

In some congregations, organizing mutual help groups for grievers has created a safe place and safe space—whether the group is continual or time limited. Grievers learn from one another rather than from experts. My experience leading groups in a local church has taught me that some will be reluctant to attend a group in their own congregation and prefer to attend a support group in another congregation or one sponsored by a hospital, funeral home, or hospice.

A grief group is only as healthy as its leadership.

Leaders who have their own agendas or who use the group to do their own grief work have hamstrung some groups from the beginning. Too many rely on the outdated "stages" theory of grief. (One resource that many groups use is *Death and Grief: Healing Through Small Groups,* Augsburg Press, 1995.)

Bereavement groups are not meant to operate in lieu of pastoral leadership and care; rather, they complement them.

> Ultimately, the group provides validation for their grief and heartache—that they are not weak or crazy—and provides them with that "safe place" to begin the grief process in a healthy way. The groups promote remembering because it is so important to do so.
> —Barbara R. Hirsch, 1998, p. 31

Some Christians avoid worship services because the setting reminds them of their loss. "I look around, and all I see is couples—that's where I feel my loss the most," one widower told our grief group. "We sat in the same pew for 30 years. Now, I feel so alone . . . and if I start crying, I feel like everyone's staring at me." Others find that eating alone on Sunday can be brutal and negate the benefits of worship. What a gift when members say to a griever, "Come and eat brunch with us"!

High noon after Sunday worship
can be the loneliest point of a week
for a widow or widower.

One young mother whose child has died and wonders what's going to happen to her marriage asks, "Why does worship *always* have to be so happy? I go to church and everyone seems happy, happy, happy! The choruses are upbeat and the sermon is upbeat. There's no place for me to be honest and to be myself."

Healthy churches work at being safe places
for grievers to be real.

In reality, in some congregations in conservative Evangelical Christianity, ongoing grief is disenfranchised. One associate pastor's daughter was killed in a car wreck. When another teen in that church, a friend of the associate's daughter, was killed in an accident 15 months later, the associate pastor's grief was reopened. However, he was chastised by the senior minister moments before the worship service began: "Can't you just put on a happy face for the people? Your daughter is with the Lord! I don't care what you do on your own time, but in worship, when you're on the platform where people can see you, you need to set a positive example." Another griever describes the "foyer" conversations after church: "Oh, yeah—they ask me how I'm doing. But they never want to stick around to hear my answer. You can tell they're really nervous around me as if grief is contagious. They all want me to be doing fine. So I just lie and mumble, 'Fine, fine. Thanks for asking.' Not once has anyone said, 'I want to know how you're *really* doing.'"

One father adds, "They just slap me on the shoulder and say, 'You're doing so well. God bless you' or 'You're just handling this so beautifully.' They never slow down enough to ask how I'm doing. I've come to the conclusion that they don't really want to know how I'm doing. All that business about 'When one has a heartache, we all shed a tear' is just a chorus—not reality—around here."

We may not be able to solve the problems of the griever. We may not comprehend the forms that must be filled out and the bureaucracy that must be dealt with. We may not be counselors. But what we have we can give. Donald Howard (1980) from his experience of grief concludes, "No one ought ever to feel alone when a member of a church" (p. 23).

How do the bereaving in your congregation define hospitality? Is grief a problem to be solved or an invitation to servanthood?

At some point, each of us will join the ranks of grievers.
In fact, it may take a direct encounter with loss
to reshape our compassion.

Pohl (1999) contends that "people learn hospitality by doing it." I would add that they also learn it by witnessing it. So what does being a contemporary Christian require? "An openness of heart, a willingness to make one's life visible to others, and a generosity of time and resources" (p. 13), basically, a willingness to be interrupted. Robert Benson (1998) contends that some Christians "do" their prayers.

As the news spread around town, people began to do the only thing they could do: they began to pray. Many of them did so with their hands. One came and sat with Mary Lou while she held Keenan and said goodbye to the sweet boy she had never really had a chance to say hello to. Another came to be on the telephone in the waiting room and make the calls that spread the word. At another telephone, another friend was beginning the process of making the arrangements, the process we have all seen and dread to think about having to do. Someone else came to stay with the other children until Gary could get home with the terrible news instead of with a new baby brother *(pp. 135-36).*

Half of hospitality is just showing up. Benson concludes, after pointing out the acts of gracious kindness and hospitality, "Together, they 'prayed' the prayer of intercession, the prayer of shouldering the burdens of others" (p. 136).

Congregations are empowered to be effective when pastors, staff, and members work to create safe places and safe spaces to grieve.

Conclusion

Good-bye is an essential part of the language of humans. The small "good-byes" are rehearsals for the moment of the grand good-bye. Through 20 centuries the Church has said, "You don't have to go through saying good-bye alone." I like the song by Ira B. Wilson titled "Make Me a Blessing." I cannot forget one line of the lyrics: "Out of my life may Jesus shine." Out of my life, my compassion, and my hospitality—congregational care is making Jesus shine in the darkness of death and grief.

It's not in the great acts of pastoral brilliance that mercy
is distributed through a local congregation. Rather,
it's through the countless, often unnoticed cups of
cold water or hot coffee given in Jesus' name.

Gerkin (1997) laments that most churches have grown too large for a pastor—even one who wants to be a shepherd—to be available to all with needs and demands. But the congregation can be mobilized, trained, and empowered to do the work of caring for the bereaved. What is needed is what early generations of Christians called "fellowship."

> **This level of care is apt to be expressed not so much in words as in an arm on the shoulder, or, in the case of bereavement, the provision of food or flowers.**
> —Charles V. Gerkin, 1997, p. 103

Goal of Pastoral Leadership

Congregations can be empowered to offer "deeds of love and mercy" to those who are grieving. A caring congregation equips saints to care sensitively for the bereaving.

A Spiritual Formation Exercise

1. Take a moment to read Luke 7:36-50, an account of lavish attention.
2. Pause. Invite God to speak to you in this encounter with Scripture.
3. Read the passage a second time—slowly. What catches your attention? Think of a way that you have been lavish with attention for a griever.
4. Pastors always have more things on their agendas than can be done in a day. Just as Jesus was criticized, our way of expressing compassion can be a subject of criticism or challenge (v. 39). How do you respond to such criticism?
5. Spend some time with this phrase: "Then he turned toward the woman and said to Simon, 'Do you see *this* woman?'" (v. 44, emphasis added). Think about the tone of voice Jesus might have used. Now try out these words in several tones of voice: "Do you see *this* griever?"
6. Ask God to show you how you see grievers.

A Leadership Decision

As a result of reading this chapter, I need to

1. _____

2. _____

A Story That Will Preach

A wonderful Chinese story tells about an elephant happening upon a hummingbird lying flat on the ground with his feet raised toward the sky. The peculiar sight invited the elephant's curiosity.

"Hummingbird!" the elephant demanded. "What are you doing with your feet up in the air?"

"I heard that the sky might fall today. If that happens, I'm just practicing doing my part to hold it up." That response produced belly laughs from the elephant.

"My dear little friend, do you honestly think those scraggily little feet could hold up the sky?"

"Oh, not alone," the hummingbird responded. "But each must do what he can. And this is what I can do."

In the days and weeks and months ahead, do what you can to soften this burden of grief.

One of the spiritually healthy things a community of faith can offer—that the world can imitate but never fully duplicate—is a safe place to do the normal work of grieving. Jesus, in His dying, did not "transfer" responsibility for His mother to one of His siblings, but rather to one of His disciples with a simple word, "Behold, your mother . . ." (John 19:27). Long after the culture has grown weary, even distanced itself, Christians keep on caring.

Bibliography

Names in bold indicate sources specifically cited in the book. Other sources were consulted and were considered important in the writing of the book.

Aaron, William F. (1999, December). Funeral service in the year 2000. *The Director*, 5.

Aaron, William F. (2000, January). My new year's challenge. *The Director*, 4.

Abbot Barnabas. (2000, 2 August). Funeral sermon, Benedictine Abbey, Atcheson, Kansas.

Albacete, Lorenzo. (2000, 27 August). Good grief and bad. *The New York Times Magazine,* Section 6, 22.

Albom, Mitch. (1997). *Tuesdays with Morrie: An old man, a young man, and life's greatest lesson.* New York: Doubleday.

Alexander, Victoria. (1991). *Words I never thought to speak: Stories of life in the wake of suicide.* New York: Lexington Books.

Andersen, Christopher. (2000). *The day John died.* New York: William Morrow.

Anderson, Herbert, and Foley, Edwards. (1997, 5 November). Experiences in need of ritual. *The Christian Century*, 1002-8.

Anderson, Leith. (1990). *Dying for change.* Minneapolis, MN: Bethany House.

Anderson, Robert C. (1985). *The effective pastor.* Chicago: Moody Press.

Anthony, Carl Sferrazza. (1990). *First ladies: The sage of the presidential wives and their power, 1789-1961.* New York: William Morrow/Quill.

Appley, Lawrence A. (1974). *Formula for success: A core concept of management.* New York: AMACOM.

Arbuckle, Gerald A. (2000). Letting go in hope: Spirituality for a chaotic world. In Robert J. Wicks (Ed.), *Handbook of spirituality for ministers, Volume 2: Perspectives for the 21st century* (pp. 120-33). New York: Paulist Press.

Aries, Philippe. (1974). *The hour of our death* (Patricia M. Ranum, Trans.). Baltimore: Johns Hopkins University.

Attig, Thomas. (2000). *The heart of grief: Death and the search for lasting love.* New York: Oxford University Press.

Banker, James R. (1988). *Death in the community: Memorialization and confraternities in an Italian commune in the late middle ages.* Athens, GA: University of Georgia Press.

Barna, George. (1993). *Today's pastors: A revealing look at what pastors are saying about themselves, their peers and the pressures they face.* Ventura, CA: Regal Books.

Barrett, Ronald Keith. (1998). Sociocultural considerations for working with blacks experiencing loss and grief. In Kenneth J. Doka and Joyce D. Davidson (Eds.), *Living with grief: Who we are, how we grieve* (pp. 83-96). Philadelphia: Bruner/Mazel.

Basilios IV, Archbishop of Jerusalem. (1991). Burial rites and practices. In Aziz S. Atiya (Ed.), *The Coptic encyclopedia* (2:425-26). New York: Macmillan.

Bass, Dorothy C. (2000). *Receiving the day: Christian practices for opening the gift of time.* San Francisco: Jossey-Bass.

Bayly, Albert F. (1961). Lord, whose love through humble service. In Bert Polman, Marilyn Kay Stulken, and James Rawlings Sydnor (Eds.), *Amazing grace: Hymn texts for devotional* use. Louisville, KY: Westminster John Knox Press, 249.

Bayly, Joseph. (1969). *View from the hearse.* Chicago: Moody.

Beattie, Melodie Lynn. (1997). *Stop being mean to yourself: A story about finding the true meaning of self-love.* San Francisco: HarperSan Francisco.

Benson, Robert. (1998). *Living prayer.* New York: Tarcher/Putnam.

Bern-Klug, Mercedes, Ekerdt, David J., Wilkinson, Deborah Schild. (1999). What families know about funeral-related costs: Implications for social work practice. *Health & Social Work, 24(2),* 128-37.

Blair, Robert. (1998). *The funeral and the wedding handbook.* Joplin, MO: College Press Publishing.

Bonhoeffer, Dietrich. (1954). *Life together* (John W. Doberstein, Trans.). New York: Harper & Row.

The book of common prayer and *administration of the sacraments and other rites and ceremonies of the church.* (1979). New York: Seabury Press.

Bradlee, Ben. (1995). *A good life: Newspapering and other adventures.* New York: Simon & Schuster.

Brener, Anne. (1993). *Mourning & Mitzvah: A guided journal for walking the mourner's path through grief to healing.* Woodstock, VT: Jewish Lights.

Breslin, Meg McSherry. (1998, 22 March). Moods of funerals changing. *The Chicago Tribune,* Section 4, 2-3.

Breyer, Chloe. (2000, August 30—September 6). Pastoral learning at Bellevue Hospital. *The Christian Century,* 862-69.

Brooks, Jane. (1999). *Midlife orphan: Facing life's changes now that your parents are gone.* New York: Berkeley Books.

Bruggemann, Walter. (1978). *Prophetic imagination.* Philadelphia: Westminster.

Burgess, Michele. (1989, May). West Coast spirits. *Alaska Airlines Magazine,* 40-44.

Burial services. (1974). In F. L. Cross and E. A. Livingstone (Eds.), *The Oxford dictionary of the Christian church* (2nd ed.) (p. 212). New York: Oxford University Press.

Caldwell, Charmaine, McGee, Marsha, and Pryor, Charles. (1998). The sympathy card as cultural assessment of American attitudes toward death, bereavement and extending sympathy: A replicated study. *Omega, 37(2),* 121-32.

Cameron, Julia. (2000). *God is no laughing matter: Observations and objections on the spiritual path.* New York: Tarcher.

Campolo, Tony. (1988). *Twenty hot potatoes Christians are afraid to touch.* Dallas, TX: Word.

Caspari, W. (1949). Burial. In *The new Schaff-Herzon encyclopedia of religious knowledge* (Vol. 2, pp. 308-9). Grand Rapids, MI: Baker Book House.

Chaffin, Kenneth. (2000, Fall). From the front porch. *Family Ministry, 14(3),* 6-7.

Changing of the guard. (2000, December). *The American Funeral Director,* 25-27.

Childers, Jeff W. (1997). Funeral practices. In Everett Ferguson (Ed.), *Encyclopedia of early Christianity* (2nd ed.) (1:443). New York: Garland Publishing.

Church of the Nazarene. (1997). *Manual,* 1997-2001. Kansas City, MO: Nazarene Publishing House.

Claypool, John. (1974). *Tracks of a fellow struggler: How to handle grief.* Waco, TX: Word.

Clinebell, Howard. (1966). *Basic types of pastoral counseling.* Nashville, TN: Abingdon.

Clinton, Catherine. (1982). *The plantation mistress: Woman's world in the old South.* New York: Bantam.

Coffin, Henry Sloane. (1997). Alex's death. In Phyllis Theroux (Ed.), *The book of eulogies* (pp. 344-47). New York: Scribner.

Cole, David. (2000, July). Singing the faith. *The Hymn, 51(3),* 24-27.

Confraternities. (1995). In Richard P. McBrien (Ed.), *The Harper Collins encyclopedia of Catholicism* (p. 351). San Francisco: HarperSan Francisco.

Cooke, Alistair. (1977). *Six men.* New York: Knopf.

Coolican, M. B, Stark, J., Doka, K. J., and Coor, C. A. (1994). Education about death, dying, & bereavement in nursing programs. *Nurse Educator, 19(6),* 1-6.

Corr, Charles A. (1993). Coping with dying: Lessons that we should and should not learn from the work of Elisabeth Kubler-Ross. *Death Studies (17),* 69-83.

Corr, Charles A. (1998-99). Disenfranchising the concept of disenfranchised grief. *Omega, 38(1),* 1-20.

Corr, Charles A. (1992). A task-based approach to coping with dying. *Omega, 24(2),* 81-94.

Corr, Charles A., Doka, Kenneth J., and Kastenbaum, Robert. (1999). Dying and its interpreters: A review of selected literature and some comments on the state of the field. *Omega, 39(4),* 239-59.

Corr, Charles A., Nabe, Clyde M., and Corr, Donna M. (1997). *Death & dying, life & living* (2nd ed.). Pacific Grove, CA: Brooks/Cole.

Creedy, Alan. (2000, May). Year 2000 state of the industry analysis. *The American Funeral Director,* 26-28.

Cremation Association of North America. (2000, January). Study of American attitudes toward ritualization and memorialization: 1999 update.

Crespo, Madeline. (1996, September). Death united Mexican-American community. *The Director,* 16, 18, 20.

Davies, Horton. (1970/1996). *Worship & theology in England.* Book I, Volume I: *From Cranmer to Hooker, 1534-1603.* Grand Rapids, MI: Eerdmans.

Davies, Horton. (1962/1996). *Worship & theology in England.* Book II, Volume IV: *From Newman to Martineau, 1850-1900.* Grand Rapids, MI: Eerdmans.

Davies, J. G. (1986). Burial: The early church. In J. G. Davies (Ed.), *The new Westminster dictionary of liturgy and worship* (p. 117). Philadelphia: Westminster.

Davies, Rupert, and Rupp, Gordon. (1965). *A history of the Methodist church in Great Britain* (Volume 1). London: Epworth Press.

Decker, Beatrice. (1973). *After the flowers have gone.* Grand Rapids, MI: Zondervan.

Defort, Edward J. (2000, October). "Time for some long-term planning." *The American Funeral Director,* 3.

DelBene, Ron, with Montgomery, Mary, and Montgomery, Herb. (1991). *From the heart.* Nashville, TN: Upper Room Books.

DeSpelder, L. A., and Strickland, L. A. (2000). The last dance: Encountering death and dying (5th ed.). Mountain View, CA: Mayfield.

DeSpelder, Lynne Anne, and Stickland, Albert Lee. (1996). *The last dance: Encountering death and dying* (4th ed.). Mountain View, CA: Mayfield Publishing.

Devore, W. (1990). The experience of death: A Black perspective. In J. K. Parry (Ed.), *Social work practice with the terminally ill: A transcultural perspective* (pp. 100-107). Springfield, IL: Charles C. Thomas.

Dissanayake, Ellen. (1995). *Homo aestheticus.* Seattle, WA: University of Washington Press.

Doka, Kenneth. (1989). Disenfranchised grief. In Kenneth Doka (Ed.), *Disenfranchised grief: Recognizing hidden sorrow* (pp. 3-11). Lexington, MA: Lexington Books.

Doka, Kenneth J., and Morgan, John D. (Eds.). (1993). *Death & spirituality.* Death, Value & Meaning Series (John D. Morgan, Series ed.). Amityville, NY: Baywood.

Doka, Kenneth J., and Davidson, Joyce (Eds.). (1998). *Living with grief: Who we are, how we grieve.* Washington, DC: Bruner/Mazel.

Donovan, Anne. (1998, 19 September). The painful effort to believe. *America,* 4-11.

Downe-Wambolt, Barbara, and Tamlyn, Deborah. (1997). An international survey of death education trends in faculties of nursing and medicine. *Death Studies,* 21, 177.

Downey, William E. (1998, 8 April). Funerals in Germany: Secular rites. *The Christian Century,* 358-59.

Dubin, W. R., and Sarnoff, J. R. (1986). Suddenly unexpected death: Intervention with survivors. *American Emergency Medicine, 15(1),* 54-57.

Dugan, Eileen T. (1996). Funerals. In Hans J. Hillerbrand (Ed.), *The Oxford encyclopedia of the Reformation* (1:151-52). New York: Oxford University Press.

Dunlop, A. I. (1993). Burial. In David F. Wright, David C. Lachman, and Donald E. Meek (Eds.), *Dictionary of Scottish church history & theology.* Downers Grove, IL: InterVarsity Press.

Eakes, Georgene G. (1990). Grief resolution in hospice nurses: An exploration of effective methods. *Nursing & Health Care, 11(5),* 243-48.

Eakes, Georgene G. (1984). The nurse/patient relationship in terminal cases: A consideration for providers of holistic care in coping with death. *Home Healthcare Nurse, 2(4),* 17-19.

Easterling, Larry W., Gamino, Louis A., Sewell, Kenneth W., & Stirman, Linda S. (2000, Fall). Spiritual experience, church attendance, and bereavement. *The Journal of Pastoral Care, 54(3),* 262-75.

Edelman, Hope. (1994, 15 May). Quoted in Grief has no beginning, middle or end. *The New York Times Book Magazine,* np.

Editors of Life. (1994). *Remembering Jackie: A life in pictures.* New York: Warner Books.

Feigenberg, L. (1980). *Terminal care: Friendship contracts with dying cancer patients* (P. Hort, Trans.). New York: Bruner/Mazel.

Fox, Karen L., and Miller, Phyllis Zimbler. (1992). *Seasons for celebration.* New York: Perigee Book.

Galloway, Dale. (2000, 21 November). Personal interview. Lexington, KY.

Gallup International Institute. (1997). *Spiritual beliefs and the dying process: A report on a national survey conducted for the Nathan Cummings Foundation and Ftezer Institute.*

George, A. Raymond. (1986). Burial: Methodist. In J. G. Davies (Ed.), *The new Westminster dictionary of liturgy and worship* (p. 127). Philadelphia: Westminster.

Gerkin, Charles V. (1997). *Introduction to pastoral counseling.* Nashville, TN: Abingdon.

Gilbert, Richard. (2001). Living, dying, and grieving in the margins. (At press). In John Morgan (Ed.), *Papers presented at King's College Conference of Bereavement.* Amityville, NY: Baywood.

Gilbert, Richard B. (1998, September). Creating ritual spaces for kids: A marketing and caring plan for funeral homes. *The Director, 70(9),* 46-47.

Gladstone, William. (1938, March). Successful cemetery advertising. *The American Cemetery,* 13.

Green, Arthur. (1999). *These are the words: A vocabulary of Jewish spiritual life.* Woodstock, VT: Jewish Lights.

Grollman, Earl A. (1993). Death in Jewish thought. In Kenneth J. Doka with John D. Morgan (Eds.), *Death and spirituality* (chap. 3, pp. 21-32). Amityville, NY: Baywood Publishing.

Grollman, Earl A. (1998). What you always wanted to know about your Jewish clients' perspectives concerning death and dying—but were afraid to ask. In Kenneth J. Doka and Joyce D. Davidson (Eds.), *Living with grief: Who we are, how we grieve* (chap. 2, pp. 27-37). Philadelphia: Bruner/Mazel.

Guest, Larry. (2000). *The Payne Stewart story.* Kansas City, MO: Woodford Press/Stark Books/Andrews McMeel.

Gurley, George. (1992, 26 October). A not so gentle reminder. *The Kansas City Star,* C-1.

Haines, Polly J. (1999, 29 July). Going back to school won't be easy for Columbine High School students. *The Florida Baptist Witness,* 8-9.

Hamilton, Adam. (2000, November/December). The six roles of a large-church pastor. *The Circuit Rider, 24(6),* 13-15.

Hanson, Karen R. (1996). Minister as midwife. *The Journal of Pastoral Care, 50(3),* 249-56.

Harbaugh, Gary. (1984). *The pastor as person.* Minneapolis, MN: Augsburg.

Harris, Audrey, and Weems, Cynthia D. (2000, November/December). Leading a small church. *The Circuit Rider, 24(6),* 8-9.

Hatchett, Marion J. (1995). *Commentary on the American Prayer Book.* New York: HarperCollins.

Hines, Paulette Moore. (1991). Death and African-American culture. In F. Walsh and M. McGoldrick (Eds.), *Living beyond loss: Death in the family* (pp. 186-91). New York: Norton.

Hirsch, Barbara A. (1997, February). Bereavement support groups: An integral component of an aftercare program. *The Director,* 29-31.

Hobgood, William Chris. (1998) *The once and future pastor: The changing role of religious leaders.* Washington, DC: The Alban Institute.

Holbrook, Bill. (2000, September). Meaningful funeral ceremonies: Poppycock or possibility? *The Director,* 36-46.

How, William Walsham. (1864/1994). For all the saints. In Bert Polman, Marilyn Kay Stulken, and James Rawlings Sydnor (Eds.), *Amazing grace: Hymn texts for devotional use.* Louisville, KY: Westminster John Knox Press, 293.

Howard, Donald. (1980). *Christians grieve too.* Carlisle, PA: Banner of Truth Trust.

Howard, Sue, and Howard, Gail. (1973). *I am afraid.* Pasadena, CA: World-Wide Missions.

Hughes, Kent, and Hughes, Barbara. (1987). *Liberating ministry from the success syndrome.* Wheaton, IL: Tyndale.

Hunter, George G., III. (2000). *Leading & managing a growing church.* Nashville, TN: Abingdon.

Hustad, Donald P. (1981). *Jubilate! Church music in the evangelical tradition.* Carol Stream, IL: Hope Publishing.

International Commission on English in the Liturgy. (1990). *Order of Christian funerals* (Rev. study ed.). Chicago: Liturgy Training Publications.

Island, Bernard. (1998). *Jane's naval history of World War II.* New York: HarperCollins.

Johnson, Elizabeth A. (1999). *Friends of God and prophets: A feminist theological reading of the communion of saints.* New York: Continuum.

Jones, Jim. (1999, 20 September). Wedgwood Baptist reclaimed for worship. *The Fort Worth Star-Telegram,* 1A, 11A.

Jung, Shannon, Boehm, Pegge, Cronin, Deborah, Farley, Gary, Freudenberger, C. Dean, La Blanc, Sandra, Queen, Edward L., II, and Ruesink, David C. (2000). *Rural ministry: The shape of renewal to come.* Nashville, TN: Abingdon.

Kahn, Robert L., and Antonucci, Toni C. (1980). Convoys over the life course: Attachment, roles, and social support. In Paul B. Baltes and Orville G. Brim, Jr. (Vol. eds.), *Life span development and behavior* (3:253-83). New York: Academic Press.

Kastenbaum, Robert. (1998). *Death, society, and human experience* (6th ed.). Boston: Allyn & Bacon.

Kavanaugh, Lee Hill. (2000, 5 September). On rural roads, clash of cultures can turn deadly. *The Kansas City Star,* A-1, A-5.

Kavanaugh, Lee Hill. (2000, 23 November). USS Cole sailor, family share holiday. *The Kansas City Star,* C-1, C-2.

Kay, Alan A. (1993). *A Jewish book of comfort.* Northvale, NJ: Jason Aronson.

Kolatch, Alfred J. (1993). *The Jewish mourner's book of why.* Middle Village, NY: Jonathan David.

Kubler-Ross, Elizabeth. (1969). *On death and dying.* New York: Macmillan.

LaFavre, Robert. (1998, 19 March). Pastor needs prayer when ministering to the bereaved. *The Florida Baptist Witness,* 3.

Lageman, August G. (1986). The emotional dynamics of funeral services. *Pastoral Psychology, 35(1),* 16-22.

Lash, Joseph P. (1971). *Eleanor: The years alone.* New York: W. W. Norton.

L'Engle, Madeleine. (1996). *Glimpses of grace: Daily thoughts and reflections.* San Francisco: HarperSan Francisco.

LesStrange, Barbara. (2000, October). Aftercare: An Interview with Ken Davey. *The American Funeral Director,* 42-48.

Lewis, C. S. (1961). *A grief observed.* New York: Bantam.

Lewis, C. S. (1946, 1966). Preface. In Dorothy Sayers, J. R. R. Tolkien, C. S. Lewis, A. O. Barfield, Gervase Mathew, and W. H. Lewis, *Essays presented to Charles Williams* (vi-xiv). Grand Rapids, MI: William B. Eerdmans.

Lewis, C. S. (1944/1962). *The problem of pain.* New York: Macmillan Paperbacks.

Lloyd, Dan S. (1997). *Leading today's funerals: A pastoral guide for improving bereavement ministry.* Grand Rapids, MI: Baker.

Lofland, L. H. (1982). In W. J. Ickes and E. S. Knowles (Eds.), *Personality, roles, and social behavior* (pp. 219-41). New York: Verlag.

Logan, Kim. (No date). Creating meaningful rituals, Handout, Kansas City, MO: Kansas City Hospice.

Long, Thomas G. (1997, October). The American funeral today—trends and issues. *The Director, 69(10),* 10-16.

Long, Thomas G. (1999). Why Jessica Mitford was wrong. *Theology Today, 55(4),* 496-509.

Lothrop, Hannah. (1997). *Help, comfort and hope after losing your baby in pregnancy or the first year.* Tucson, AZ: Fisher Books.

Lunn, Carolyn. (1992). *Joy—Anyway!* Kansas City, MO: Beacon Hill Press of Kansas City.

Lyman, Rebecca. (1999). *Early Christian traditions.* Boston: Cowley Publications.

Lynch, Thomas. (1999, October). Making the world safe for McFunerals. *The Director, 71(10),* 94, 96, 98.

Lynch, Thomas. (1997). *The undertaking: Life studies from the dismal trade.* New York: Norton.

Magida, Arthur J. (Ed.). (1996). *How to be a perfect stranger: A guide to etiquette in other people's religious ceremonies.* Volume 1. Woodstock, VT: Jewish Lights Publications.

Manning, Brennan. (2000). *Ruthless trust: The ragamuffin's path to God.* San Francisco: HarperSan Francisco.

Manning, Doug. (1979). *Don't take my grief away.* San Francisco: Harper & Row.

Mansell, John S. (1998). *The funeral: A pastor's guide.* Nashville, TN: Abingdon.

Martin, Judith. (1999, 18 April). Miss Manners: Funerals are beyond compare. *The Dallas Morning News,* 5E.

Matlins, Stuart M., and Magida, Arthur J. (Eds.). (1997). *How to be a perfect stranger: A guide to etiquette in other people's religious ceremonies.* Volume 2. Woodstock, VT: Jewish Lights Publications.

Mathewes-Green, Frederica. (1999). *At the corner of East and now.* New York: Jeremy T. Tarcher.

Maxwell, John C. (1998). *The 21 irrefutable laws of leadership: Follow them and people will follow you.* Nashville, TN: Thomas Nelson.

Mayne, Michael. (1998). *Pray, love, remember.* London: Darton, Longman, & Todd.

McClintock, John, and Staff, James. (1891). Dead, prayers for the dead. In *Cyclopedia of biblical, theological and ecclesiastical literature* (2:710). New York: Harper & Brothers.

McConnell, Stephen D. (1998). Christians in grief. In Kenneth J. Doka and Joyce C. Davidson (Eds.), *Living with grief: Who we are, how we grieve* (chap. 3, pp. 39-46). Philadelphia: Bruner/Mazel.

McCormick, Mac. (2000, August). The broken necklace. *The American Funeral Director,* 78.

McCormick, Mac. (2000, May). A personal touch. *The American Funeral Director,* 20-23.

McCullough, David. (1992). *Truman.* New York: Simon & Schuster.

McCullough, Melvin. (1999, 9 April). Statement to congregation. First Church of the Nazarene, Bethany, OK.

McGoldrick, Monica. (1991). Irish families. In F. Walsh and M. McGoldrick (Eds.), *Living beyond loss: Death in the family* (pp. 179-82). New York: W. W. Norton.

McKinnis, Rick. (1987). Preparing the congregation for death. In *Weddings, funerals, and special events.* Carol Stream, IL: Cti/Word (pp. 69-80).

McLean, Andrew M. (1996). Death. In Hans J. Hillerbrand (Ed.), *The Oxford encyclopedia of the Reformation* (1:468-69). New York: Oxford University Press.

Meador, Keith G., and Jones, Gregory. (2000, 16-23 August). Bearing witness in life & death. *The Christian Century,* 831-32.

Meeks, Wayne A. (1983). *The first urban Christians: The social world of the apostle Paul.* New Haven, CT: Yale University Press.

Merton, Thomas (Ed.). (1965). *Gandhi on non-violence: Selected texts from Mohandas K. Gandi's non-violence in peace and war.* New York: New Directions.

Metcalf, Peter, and Huntington, Richard. (1991). *Celebrations of death: The anthropology of mortuary ritual* (2nd ed.). New York: Cambridge University Press.

Miller, James E. (2000). *When mourning dawns.* Fort Wayne, IN: Willowgreen Publications.

Mirabella, Jennifer. (2000, October). Business advantage of the month: The end of euphemisms. *The Director,* 72(10), 22.

Moe, Thomas. (1997). *Pastoral care in pregnancy loss: A ministry long needed.* New York: Haworth Pastoral Press.

Morgan, E. (1994). Bereavement. In J. Morgan (Ed.), *Dealing creatively with death: A manual of death education & simple burial.* New York: Zinn Communications.

Morgan, Ernest. (1988). Bereavement. In Jenifer Morgan (Ed.), *Dealing creatively with death: A manual of death education & simple burial.* New York: Zinn Communications.

Murphy, N. Michael. (1999). *The wisdom of dying: Practices for living.* Boston: Element.

Neeld, Elizabeth Harper. (1990). *Seven choices: Taking the steps to a new life after losing someone you love.* New York: Delta/Dell.

Neimeyer, Robert A. (1998). *Lessons of loss: A guide to coping.* New York: McGraw-Hill/Primis Custom Publishing.

Nelsen, Vivian Jenkins. (1998). One woman's interracial journey. In Alicia Skinner Cook and Kevin Ann Oltjenbruns (Eds.), *Dying and grieving: Life span and family perspectives* (2nd ed.) (pp. 24-30). Fort Worth, TX: Harcourt Brace College Publishers.

Niebergall, A., and Lathrop, Gordon. (1986). Burial: Lutheran. In J. G. Davies (Ed.), *The new Westminster dictionary of liturgy and worship* (pp. 124-27). Philadelphia: Westminster.

No man is poor who has friends. (1997, 8 July). *The Kansas City Star,* A.

Nuland, Sherwin B. (1994). *How we die: Reflections on life's final chapter.* New York: Knopf.

Oates, Wayne. (1982). *The Christian pastor* (3rd ed., rev.). Philadelphia: Westminster.

Oden, Thomas C. (1983). *Pastoral theology: Essentials of ministry.* San Francisco: Harper & Row.

Oltjenbruns, Kevin. (1995, April). Building friendships during childhood: Significance of the death of a peer. Paper presented at the meeting of the Association for Death Education and Counseling, Miami.

Parachin, Victor. (2000, October). Going it alone. *The Director, 72(10),* 14, 16.

Parrott, Les, III (1999). Grieving the death of a spouse. *Journal of Psychology and Christianity, 18(4),* 330-37.

Pattison, E. M. (1998). *The experience of dying.* Englewood Cliffs, NJ: Prentice-Hall.

Perret, Geoffrey. (1999). *Eisenhower.* New York: Random House.

Peterson, Eugene H. (2000). *The Message: Old Testament Prophets.* Colorado Springs, CO: NavPress.

Pohl, Christine D. (1999). *Making room: Rediscovering hospitality as a Christian tradition.* Grand Rapids, MI: Eerdmans.

Pokorski, Doug. (1995). *Death rehearsal: A practical guide for preparing for the inevitable.* Springfield, IL: Octavio Press.

Pollock, John. (1989). *John Wesley.* Wheaton, IL: Victor Books.

Post, Elizabeth L. (1992). *Emily Post's etiquette* (15th ed). New York: HarperCollins.

Potter, Donald L. (2000, October). Marketing to a changing world. *American Funeral Director,* 21, 81.

Rabbinical Assembly. (1998). *Siddur Sim Shalom for Shabbat and festivals.* [No place of publication identified.] The United Synagogue of Conservative Judaism.

Raether, Howard. (1999, September). Death, the funeral home & the funeral practitioner. *The Director, 71(9),* 26, 28.

Raether, Howard. (1997, November). Deaths and cremations—1995, 1996 and beyond. *The Director, 69(11),* 77-78.

Raether, Howard C. (1998, April). Thirty years in funeral service. *The Director,* 81.

Rah, Soong-Chan. (2000, Fall). Navigating cultural currents. *Leadership,* 39-42.

Rando, Therese A. (1984). *Grief, dying, and death: Clinical interventions for caregivers.* Champaign, IL: Research Press.

Rando, Therese A. (1992-93). The increasing prevalence of complicated mourning: The onslaught is just beginning. *Omega, 26(1),* 43-59.

Reynolds, William J. (1990). *Songs of glory: Stories of 300 great hymns and gospel songs.* Grand Rapids, MI: Zondervan.

Ridlehoover, Jack. (1995, June). Working with the funeral director. *Church Administration, 37(9)*, 14-16.

Rocco, Stephen R. (1998, March). Legal rights to a deceased's burial: Who decides? *The Director, 70(3)*, 68-74.

Rogal, Samuel J. (1998). *A biographical dictionary of 18th century Methodism* (Volume 4). Lewison, England: The Edwin Mellen Press.

Rogness, Alvin N. (1999). *When you are suffering: A book of comfort.* Minneapolis, MN: Augsburg.

Rohr, Richard. (1999). *Everything belongs: The gift of contemplative prayer.* Notre Dame, IN: Ava Maria Press.

Rosten, Leo. (1977). *Leo Rosten's treasury of Jewish quotations.* New York: Bantam.

Rupp, Joyce. (1988). *Praying our goodbyes.* Notre Dame, IN: Ava Maria Press.

Rush, A. C. (1969). Burial, II (early Christian). In *New Catholic encyclopedia* (2:894-986). San Francisco: McGraw-Hill.

Russell, Brent. (1996, October). Joseph of Arimathaea: The patron saint of funeral directors. *The Director,* 56, 58.

Russell, Mary Andres. (2000, October). Meaning, flexibility and a hook. *American Funeral Director*, 20-21, 80-81.

Rutherford, Richard. (1980). *The death of a Christian: The rite of funerals.* New York: Pueblo Publishing.

Sanders, Catherine. (1998). Gender differences in bereavement expression across the life span. In Kenneth J. Doka and Joyce D. Davidson (Eds.), *Living with grief: Who we are, how we grieve* (pp. 121-32). Philadelphia: Bruner/Mazel.

Sanders, Catherine. (1995). The grief of children and parents. In Kenneth J. Doka (Ed.), *Children mourning, Mourning children* (pp. 69-84). Washington, DC: Hospice Foundation of America/Taylor & Francis.

Saxer, V. (1992). Dead, cult of the. In Angelo Di Bernardino (Ed.), *Encyclopedia of the early church* (1:221-22) (A. Walford, Trans.). New York: Oxford University Press (Original work published 1992).

Schaller, Lyle E. (1999). *Discontinuity and hope: Radical change and the path to the future.* Nashville, TN: Abingdon.

Schubiner, Howard. (1991, June). How to identify the suicidal teen. *Medical Aspects of Human Sexuality,* 51-52.

Scott, Douglas G. (2000, Fall). When the unchurched want a church wedding. *Leadership,* 115-20.

Searl, Edward. (2000). *In memoriam: A guide to modern funeral and memorial services* (2nd ed.). Boston: Skinner House Books.

Searl, Edward. (1993). *In memoriam: A guide to modern funeral and memorial services* Boston: Skinner House Books.

Sheehy, Sandy. (2000). *Connecting: The enduring power of female friendship.* New York: Morrow/American Psychiatric Press.

Shelley, Marshall. (2000, Fall). Broader pastures, more breeds. *Leadership,* 33-34.

Shneidman, E. S. (1980/1995). *Voices of death.* New York: Harper & Row/Kodansha International.

Shriver, Maria. (1999). *What's heaven?* New York: Golden Books.

Sims, Darcie. (2000). Rituals right or rituals ruined: The secrets to successful memorial programs. Presentation, Association for Death Education and Counseling, Charlotte.

Sittser, Gerald L. (1995). *A grace disguised: How the soul grows through loss.* Grand Rapids, MI: Zondervan.

Sly, Randy. (1993, June/July/August). What I learned about caring from funeral directors. *The Preacher's Magazine,* 17-19.

Smith, Harold Ivan. (1999). *A Decembered grief: living with loss when others are celebrating.* Kansas City, MO: Beacon Hill Press of Kansas City.

Smith, Harold Ivan. (2000, July-August). Friendgrief: The consequence of friending. *Forum, 26(4),* 1, 3-4.

Smith, Harold Ivan. (1996). *Grieving the death of a friend.* Minneapolis, MN: Augsburg.

Smith, Harold Ivan. (1994). *On grieving the death of a father.* Minneapolis, MN: Augsburg.

Smith, Harold Ivan. (1993). The impact of a storytelling seminar for friend-grievers. Unpublished D.Min. dissertation-project, Asbury Theological Seminary.

Smith, William, and Cheetham, Samuel (Eds.). (1875). Burial of the dead. In *A dictionary of Christian antiquities* (1:251-54). Boston: Little Brown.

Stannard, David R. (1977). *The Puritan way of death: A study of religion, culture, and social change.* New York: Oxford University Press.

Stannard, David R. (1975). *Death and dying in central Appalachia.* Philadelphia: University of Pennsylvania Press.

Steinsaltz, Adin. (1999). *Simple words: Thinking about what really matters in life.* E. Schachter and D. Shabtai (Eds.). New York: Simon & Schuster.

Stowe, Eugene L. (1976). *The ministry of shepherding: A study of pastoral practice.* Kansas City, MO: Beacon Hill Press of Kansas City.

Stroebe, Margaret. (1992-93). Coping with bereavement: A review of the grief work hypothesis. *Omega, 26(1),* 19-42.

Stuart, Elizabeth (Ed.). (1992). *Daring to speak love's name: A gay and lesbian prayer book.* London: Hamish Hamilton.

Swicegood, Terry. (2000, Fall). Parson: Deliberate downsizing. *Leadership,* 27-28.

Swift, John. (2000). In the hospital. In Gary Ahlskogl (Ed.), *Guide to pastoral counseling and care* (pp. 177-208). Madison, CT: Psychosocial Press.

Syme, Daniel B. (1988). *The Jewish home: A guide for Jewish living.* New York: Union of American Hebrew Congregations.

Tennessee casket store law ruled unconstitutional. (2000, October). *The American Funeral Director,* 8-9, 12.

Theroux, Phyllis. (1990, 21 October). The life and death of a mayor. *The Washington Post,* C5.

Thomas, Zach. (1994). *Healing touch: The church's forgotten language.* Louisville, KY: Westminster/John Knox Press.

Toler, Stan. (1996). *Minute motivators: Instant insight for leaders.* Kansas City, MO: Beacon Hill Press of Kansas City.

Trillin, Calvin. (1993). *Remembering Denny.* New York: Farrar, Straus, Giroux.

Turner, V. (1977). *The ritual process.* Ithica, NY: Cornell University Press.

The United Methodist Book of Worship. (1992). Nashville, TN: The United Methodist Publishing House.

The United Methodist Church. (1989). *The United Methodist hymnal: Book of the United Methodist worship.* Nashville, TN: United Methodist Publishing House.

Unruh, D. (1983). Death and personal history: Strategies of identity preservation. *Social Problems, 30(3),* 340-51.

Upton, Julia. (1990). Burial, Christian. In Peter E. Fink (Ed.). *The new dictionary of sacramental worship* (pp. 140-49). Collegeville, MN: The Liturgical Press.

USA is a mobile nation. (2000, 6 December). *USA Today,* 1A.

Valdiserri, Ronald O. (1994). *Gardening in clay: Reflections on AIDS.* Ithaca, NY: Cornell Univ. Press.

Van Beck, Todd W. (2000, May). Biblical references to the issue of funeralization. *The American Funeral Director,* 62, 64.

Van Beck, Todd W. (2000, March). The fossores: Our early funeral directors and cemeterians. Funerals in the Bible. *The American Funeral Director,* 60-61.

Van Beck, Todd. (1998, April). The future of funeral service. *The Director, 69(4),* 8, 10, 12.

Van Beck, Todd W. (1997, September). Why people like funeral directors. *The Director, 69(9),* 76-77.

Van Biema, David. (1999, 31 May). A surge of teen spirit. *Time,* 58-59.

Vanezis, Maria, and McGee, Anna. (1999). Mediating factors in the grieving process of the suddenly bereaved. *The British Journal of Nursing, 8(14),* 932-37.

van Gennep, A. (1960). *The rites of passage.* Chicago: University of Chicago Press.

Walczak, Kathleen. (2000, November). Consumers have spoken. *The Director,* 26-27.

Walfoort, Nina. (1998, 27 November). Newcomers fuel increase in housing, services. *The Louisville Courier Journal,* A-1, A-5.

Wall, James M. (1997, 24 September—1 October). Grief and loss: A death observed. *The Christian Century,* 819.

Walmsley, Roberta Chapin, and Lummis, Adair T. (1997). *Healthy clergy, wounded healers: Their families and their ministries.* New York: Church Publishing Inc.

Walter, Tony. (1999). *On Bereavement: The culture of grief.* Philadelphia: Open University Press.

Webster's *ninth new collegiate dictionary.* (1983). Springfield, MA: Merriam-Webster.

Weisman, A. D. (1977). *On dying and denying: A psychiatric study of terminality.* New York: Behavioral Publications.

Weiss, Hali. (1997, 10 September). Loosening the rules of mourning. *The Los Angeles Times,* A11.

Welshons, John E. (2000). *Awakening from grief: Finding the road back to joy.* Little Falls, NJ: Open Heart Publications.

White, James F. (1980/1990). *Introduction to Christian Worship* (Rev. ed.). Nashville, TN: Abingdon.

White, L. Michael. (1990). Burial. In E. Ferguson (Ed.), *Encyclopedia of early Christianity* (pp. 161-63). New York: Garland Publishing.

White, Susan J. (1994). *Christian worship: Technological change.* Nashville, TN: Abingdon.

Whyte, David. (1995). *Fire in the earth.* Langley, WA: Many Rivers Press.

Wieseltier, Leon. (1998). *Kaddish.* New York: Knopf.

Wilcock, Penelope. (1996). *Spiritual care of dying and bereaved people.* Harrisburg, PA: Morehouse.

Williams, Mary Grace. (2000, October). All Souls' Day at St. John's. *The Evangelist,* published by Church of Saint John the Evangelist, Flossmoor, IL, 7.

Williamson, G. B. (1952). *Overseers of the flock.* Kansas City, MO: Beacon Hill Press.

Willimon, William H. (2000). *Calling & character: Virtues of the ordained life.* Nashville, TN: Abingdon.

Willis, Paul E. (1978). *Profane culture.* London: Routledge and Paul Keson.

Wiltshire, Susan Ford. (1994). *Seasons of grief and grace: A sister's story of AIDS.* Nashville, TN: Vanderbilt University Press.

Wolfe, Ben, and Jordan, Jack. (2000). Ramblings from the trenches: A clinical perspective on thanatological research. *Death Studies,* 24, 569-84.

Wolfelt, Alan D. (1995, September/October). The child's bereavement: Caregiver as gardener: A parable. *The Forum Newsletter, 21(5)*, 1, 18.

Wolfelt, Alan D. (1998, November/December). Companioning versus treating: Beyond the medical model of bereavement caregiving: Part 3. *The Forum, 24(6)*, 3, 15.

Wolfelt, Alan D. (1995, 26 October). Creating meaningful funeral ceremonies. Lecture, Kanas City, MO.

Wolfelt, Alan D. (1994). *Creating meaningful funeral ceremonies: A guide for caregivers.* Fort Collins, CO: Companion Press.

Wolfelt, Alan D. (1998, June). Creating meaningful funeral ceremonies: Part 1: Their purpose. *The Director, 70(6)*, 18-22.

Wolfelt, Alan D. (2000, October). Customer care: Location, location, location. *The Director, 72(18)*, 18, 20.

Wolfelt, Alan D. (1988). *Death and grief: A guide for clergy.* Muncie, IN: Accelerated Development.

Wolfelt, Alan D. (1997). *The journey through grief.* Fort Collins, CO: Compassion Press.

Wolfelt, Alan D. (1997, Winter). The journey through grief: The mourner's six "reconciliation" needs. *Real Life*, 36-37.

Wolfelt, Alan D. (1994, Fall). The trend toward deritualization of the funeral. *Thanos*, 4-8.

Wolfelt, Alan D. (1994, October). The waning of the funeral ritual. *The Director*, 52-58.

Woodward, Kenneth L. (1999, 14 June). The making of a martyr. *Newsweek*, 64.

Woodward, Kenneth L. (1997, 22 September). The ritual solution. *Newsweek, 62.*

Worden, J. William. (1991). *Grief counseling and grief therapy: A handbook for the mental health practitioner* (2nd ed.). New York: Springer.

Wright, J. H. (1967). Dead, prayers for the. In *The new Catholic encyclopedia* (4:672-73). New York: McGraw-Hill.

Wright, John W. (Ed.). (1998). *The New York Times 1998 almanac.* New York: The New York Times Publishing.

Wyse, Lois. (1995). *Women make the best friends.* New York: Simon & Schuster.

York, Sarah. (2000). *Remembering well: Rituals for celebrating life and mourning death.* San Francisco: Jossey-Bass.

Zedek, Michael. (1999, 22 September). Ritual. A Matter of Life and Death Conference. Compassionate Sabbath Task Force Conference sponsored by Midwest Center for Bioethics. Kansas City, MO.